Library of
Davidson College

# Rauschenbusch:

# The Formative Years

JUDSON PRESS, VALLEY FORGE

RAUSCHENBUSCH: THE FORMATIVE YEARS

Copyright © 1976
Judson Press, Valley Forge, PA 19481

All rights reserved. No part of this publication may be reproduced, stored in a retrieval system, or transmitted in any form or by any means, electronic, mechanical, photocopying, recording, or otherwise, without the prior permission of the copyright owner, except for brief quotations included in a review of the book.

**Library of Congress Cataloging in Publication Data**

Jaehn, Klaus Juergen.
   Rauschenbusch, the formative years.

   A revision of the author's thesis (Master of Divinity) which was first published in two parts in Foundations, Oct.-Dec., 1973, v. 16, no. 4 and Jan.-Mar., 1974, v. 17, no. 1.
   Bibliography: p. 49
   1. Rauschenbusch, Walter, 1861-1918. I. Title.
BX6495.R3J3   1976   230'.6'10924 [B]   75-38191
ISBN 0-8170-0707-5

Printed in the U.S.A.

The material in this book was first published in two parts in *Foundations*, October-December, 1973, Volume XVI, No. 4, © 1973, and January-March, 1974, Volume XVII, No. 1, © 1974. Copyright by the American Baptist Historical Society and reprinted by permission.

# Foreword

One morning in the fall of 1970 Klaus Jaehn walked into my office at the American Baptist Seminary of the West in Berkeley, California. He introduced himself as a German Baptist who had been in the United States only a few months. He had come to Berkeley, where Baptists were part of the rich ecumenical center in the Graduate Theological Union, to complement the seminary training that he had received in his homeland. Here, he would follow a program of theological studies which would further prepare him for ordination into the Christian ministry. He wanted me to understand that his pastoral ministry would take place in Germany. But for now, at least, he was an American seminarian; he wanted to probe the American theological mind.

Klaus was convinced that Americans had made their best contributions to the larger theological world in the field of social ethics. Almost always the Americans had learned their biblical and systematic theology from continental Europeans and perhaps a little from the British, he thought. But in the realm of the social sciences applied to theology and Christian ethics, Old World church leaders could look to their New World counterparts for insights. Even the great works of Max Weber and Ernst Troeltsch did not diminish the importance of American accomplishments in this area. These accomplishments could best be described as the practical application of social ethical theology. Above all, the American social gospel movement had reached the heart of church life and brought theology to bear on the harsh realities of twentieth-century urban life.

I thought of Walter Rauschenbusch, the "lonely prophet" of the social gospel. He was a second-generation German-American Baptist. He had studied in Europe and England as well as in America. He had pastored an inner city church and taught in a major theological seminary. Rauschenbusch's combination of evangelical commitment, social passion, academic discipline, and intellectual creativity might catch the imagination of a young German seminarian studying social ethics in America.

Klaus Jaehn's critical study of the early life and writings of Walter Rauschenbusch is the visible demonstration of how forcefully the latter caught the imagination of the former. As a participant in a movement of young German evangelical Christians with a burning concern for social reformation today, Klaus found in Rauschenbusch a model in his own tradition. Rauschenbusch was an imperfect model, to be sure (Klaus would appreciate some of the neoorthodox criticism of the earlier social gospel liberalism), but an exciting model whose subsequent influence has ranged far beyond American Christianity.

Rauschenbusch is one of those rare Christian personalities with whom all students of American religious history must reckon and one of the handful of American Christian thinkers who have made an impact in Christian circles around the world. His books are the classic literary expression of the American social gospel movement. He alone among the pre-World War I proponents of the social gospel merits Reinhold Niebuhr's critical admiration. Martin Luther King, Jr., the social gospel prophet of modern America, found inspiration in Walter Rauschenbusch.

So it was that Klaus Jaehn found incentive to take the Greyhound bus during holiday and summer seasons to visit the Rauschenbusch archives in Sioux Falls, South Dakota, and Rochester, New York. Only as a labor of love could he afford the time it took to decipher Rauschenbusch's German shorthand. But it resulted in a remarkable Master of Divinity thesis, later published as two articles in *Foundations* (October-December, 1973, and January-March, 1974), and now appearing in this book form. This is a significant contribution to the growing list of scholarly studies of the life and thought of Walter Rauschenbusch.

Eldon G. Ernst
Berkeley, California

# Table of Contents

| | |
|---|---|
| Part I | 7 |
| Part II | 36 |
| List of Resources | 49 |
| Footnotes | 53 |

# PART I

INTEREST IN WALTER RAUSCHENBUSCH has been steadily increasing in recent years. A number of his works have been brought to the attention of the broader public, either for the first time or in greater detail. Both his most important books are now available in paperback reprints. The *Rauschenbusch Reader*[1] and Robert T. Handy's *The Social Gospel in America*[2] contain essays by Rauschenbusch originally published in a great variety of sources. In 1968, Max L. Stackhouse was able to publish a manuscript which had remained undiscovered until then and which probably dates from 1891 or 1892.[3] In the preface to this book Robert T. Handy writes: "In view of the continuing significance of Rauschenbusch's social ethical theory and practice, there has been increasing interest not only in his well-known major books but also in his lesser known articles, addresses and occasional pieces."[4] Beverly Harrison, professor at Union Theological Seminary, in a review of the same book, describes this renewed interest as follows: "Younger German scholars, heirs to a tradition profoundly disdainful of American ecclesiastical activism, have begun to study his work; and a new wave of Rauschenbusch scholarship is emerging."[5]

Nevertheless, throughout the years German students in America have frequently given evidence of how fruitful Rauschenbusch's influence can be; for example, Dietrich Bonhoeffer[6] and Reinhart Müller, the author of the only German monograph on Rauschenbusch.[7]

Ray S. Baker[8] published the first essay on Rauschenbusch in 1909. Since then many articles and several books and dissertations on Rauschenbusch have followed. Yet, neither the historical nor the theological aspects of Rauschenbusch's heritage have been fully covered. His German writings especially have received very slight consideration, even though it is of primary importance. Much of Rauschenbusch's life and work took place in a German setting. He served as a minister of a German Baptist congregation in New York City for 11 years. He taught in the German section of the Seminary at Rochester, where pastors for German

Baptist congregations were trained for service on the North American continent as well as for similar groups of emigrants in other parts of the world. Even after having become a member of the English section of the Seminary, Rauschenbusch remained a faithful member of one of the German Baptist congregations of Rochester. All through his life he felt a strong solidarity with the community in which he had grown up. In light of this solidarity, it is not surprising that he wanted to share his awakening concern for social conditions with the German Baptist congregations and their preachers. This social emphasis is evidenced by his articles published between 1888 and the spring of 1891 in *Der Sendbote*, the official publication of the German Baptist churches in America. In these articles we observe the development of his understanding of Christian socialism. For this reason, these German articles are worthy of detailed scrutiny.

The period of interest for us is delimited by two particular events in Rauschenbusch's life: the beginning of his service as pastor in a slum community in New York City, in 1886, and his trip to England and Germany to study sociology and the New Testament, in 1891.

The best-known biography of Rauschenbusch is that by Dores R. Sharpe.[9] The period, however, which is of special interest to this paper, is described in greater detail in Vernon P. Bodein's *The Social Gospel of Walter Rauschenbusch and Its Relation to Religious Education*.[10] This work is of a much more biographical nature than its title indicates. Later works largely base their facts concerning Rauschenbusch's life on these two books. But since some of the facts cited have at times been misunderstood,[11] it seems necessary to give a thorough accounting of the events which affected Rauschenbusch between 1886 and 1891.

## Called to Service

Walter's father, August Rauschenbusch, had received a comprehensive university education in Germany. He was considered the most erudite German Baptist in America. He considered his son Walter to be extraordinarily talented and felt obliged to afford him all available educational opportunities.[12] Accordingly, Walter was sent to the "Free Academy" at Rochester, then to the *gymnasium* at Gütersloh in Germany from which he graduated as *primus omnium*. He then studied at the University of Rochester and at the German and later at the English section of the Seminary in Rochester. At times he was studying simultaneously at the three last mentioned institutions. In 1886, when he had passed his final academic examinations, he was already considered by certain segments of German Baptists to be worthy of his learned father's name. He accepted a call by the Second German Baptist Church of New York and in so doing caused great wonderment among his fellow German Baptists who considered the New York church unsuitable for his qualifications. The New York congregation saw this as "a miracle before our eyes." [13] Sharpe reports that Rauschenbusch had first received an offer from a larger English-speaking church in Springfield, Illinois, but that "they were not willing to give me time for consideration at Springfield, so that the matter collapsed and I have accepted a call *received later* from the Second German Church in New York City." [14] He had been one of the first in his class who had received and accepted a call from a congregation.[15] Rauschenbusch himself described his congregation with these words:

> The congregation consists of about 130 members. But of course this means that a much larger number are under my pastoral care and under no-one else's. Almost all of them live on the West Side in the large tenement houses where often 25 families live in one building. There are some among them who have some means; most of them are simple working people; among them there are about 28 widows. The church [building] is already about 30 years old, quite ugly, and built in an inefficient way, in an unpleasant neighborhood where our evening meetings are often disturbed by noise. The younger members are intent on building a new church. I have to restrain them until the congregation is in somewhat better financial conditions.
> 
> Under the leadership of an elderly minister, the religious spirit was almost dying out. He wanted to be everybody's friend and did not achieve much.[16]

To his friend Munson Ford he wrote: "The Church has had bad experiences with my predecessors who have left an unsavory reputation behind them. The consequence is that there are many little splits and much big discouragement." [17] It could be that the reason for calling on this young educated man and for his acceptance of the call "to the crowded and sinful New York" [18] was the confused prehistory of the congregation. He wanted a challenge, and they were willing to give one.

In the beginning his annual salary amounted to $600.00 and free living quarters in the church building. These rooms were much too damp and injurious to health, so he asked that they provide another place to live. They then gave him an additional three hundred dollars to cover rent for an apartment. Since 1884 he had had health problems which developed into chronic complaints affecting his vision and hearing. At the beginning of his service in New York his condition worsened so much that he was unable to write, because of "eye trouble." [19] In June, 1886, he had to consult an ear specialist ten times. The latter also diagnosed nervous disturbances and attempted to cure them.[20] Rauschenbusch foresaw that "the time may come when I am cut off from intercourse with people and when I will have to handle only books; that's why I am now wrenching from time all it has to give." As a consequence he got completely absorbed in his pastoral work:

> I liked my work better than I had ever expected. I enjoyed everything because in everything I did I felt I was achieving something good. It was as if I had stepped from

a land of shadows into bright sunshine when I came out of the artificial circumstances of seminary life into the whirl of New York. Here things are tangible. Here one feels the waves of human life all around, as it really is, not as it ought to be according to the *decretum absolutum* of an old theology. Here one can test oneself whether the people have needs which cannot be satisfied by the almighty dollar, whether the Gospel of Jesus Christ contains a real power which could save a certain man who opens up to its influences. In a rather odd situation I will be in touch with Americans and with Germans, with the rich and with the poor. For further studies there will be little time; I don't mind that. In June I have not read anything except newspapers and yet, I have learned more than in a long time before.[21]

Rauschenbusch inaugurated his pastorate with a sermon on the theme "Your Kingdom Come" as being "the prayer to the realization of which every Christian community is called."[22] He was very busy during his first month. Apart from the usual welcoming ceremonies and the weekly assemblies, he called on every member of his congregation in their homes. At the end of the month he left New York for a two-months vacation.[23]

During these two months, and later for two months in 1887, F. W. C. Meyer, who was still a student at the Seminary in Rochester, took Rauschenbusch's place in New York. Later he was also Rauschenbusch's colleague at the Seminary. He had the following observations to make:

> In the beginning some of the good people at 45th Street believed that they had asked for a somewhat too intellectual young theologian who right away needed two months vacation in order to continue his studies. But soon they changed their opinion, and young and old was enthusiastic about his assemblies.[24]

Rauschenbusch spent his vacation time with his friend and classmate W. L. Munger at Rushford, New York.[25] He actually devoted most of his time to theological studies. He had taken along some very interesting material: about *The Life of Maurice*, he wrote:

> For a long time I had wanted to read it. He and all those of his school, Coleridge, Kingsley, F. W. Robertson, etc. are very much to my liking. To the last mentioned I owe more than to any other writer. Coleridge, too, has meant much to me. I think that we have, here in America, a theological movement closely related to theirs. But more about this later.[26]

We would wish that he would not stop at this point since his list of names creates a problem. It is true that Maurice had been influenced by Coleridge[27] and that he admired Robertson,[28] but there is no justification for speaking of a "movement." It seems that Rauschenbusch knew best those two men who had the least to do with the appearance of Christian Socialism. What he meant when he mentioned "American movement" is not clarified, neither in this place nor later. We do learn, however, that he was very familiar with the main representatives of English Christian Socialism from the very beginning of his career.

## Finding His Place

It is probable that it was during this vacation that he published his first theological work, the review of a book on church history.[29] Before that, some small poems of his had been published in magazines. In 1884 he published a substantial report on the work of the German Baptists in America.[30] In spite of this, the above-mentioned review deserves to be considered his first theological contribution. In April, 1887, another book review was published, again on a work concerning church history.[31] Rauschenbusch says that he wrote this second review at his father's suggestion, and he did not think that what he had written was very good.[32] His self-appraisal deserves to be contradicted since the review shows clearly his writing ability and his interest in ecclesiastical history.[33]

Toward the end of his vacation he experienced some very eventful weeks. He suffered from severe headaches, and he finally had to undergo a delicate eye operation. Then his ability to hear declined.[34]

At that time his sister, Emma Rauschenbusch, was a missionary in India. Starting in the fall of 1883, she was working under the supervision of the well-known Telugu missionary John E. Clough at Ongole.[35] Clough asked the Baptist Missionary Society of Boston to send Walter Rauschenbusch to the seminary at Ramapatnam in India to take the post of inspector. This request was made during Rauschenbusch's vacation. The Missionary Society was unable to make a prompt decision, mainly because the Society's secretary was in Europe at that time. Rauschenbusch's answer was that he would agree to such a post if he could be given a decisive answer by the end of September, otherwise he would prefer to work in his congregation.[36] It is probable that he was acting also on his physician's advice. F. W. C. Meyer at first felt that Rauschenbusch's health was a major factor in his not accepting the Ramapatnam post,[37] but later he maintained that his problems had arisen due to the objections of his Old Testament teacher, who had voiced doubts as to Rauschenbusch's orthodoxy.[38] This opinion was immediately repeated by others who ought to have known better. Thus questions as to his orthodoxy may have become prevalent.[39] Whatever the actual situation may have been, it is difficult to reconstruct it now.[40] In any case the outcome does not seem to have been surprising to the candidate for he wrote, "If they don't want to have me very urgently, then I don't want to go at all; because in that case they are able to find someone else rather easily and don't need to take me away from here."[41]

What was more problematic for him was the fact that he had difficulties in accepting the established religious truths as he was expected to do, namely, as a Baptist minister. He was to be ordained in October, and before that he had to submit to an interrogation by a council called to examine his beliefs. It was perhaps his parents who felt greater tension and concern than he. At that time his father wrote in a letter to Germany:

> On October 14 he will be examined by the German and the English preachers of New York in order to be ordained by them. The examination will most probably be concerned with his orthodox beliefs. In this situation it is a lucky circumstance for him that he has so far kept his doubts and deviant attitudes to himself. . . . It causes me great pain that his doubts concern mainly the *Old Testament*. Had he inherited my own way of thinking, he would express his doubts—if he had to have doubts—in some other area. . . . I once heard him remark on the prophet Ezekiel in a way which caused me pain. It was in substance the question, "what does it mean to us? Only a small part of the book offers Christian teaching!" His liking for the Old Testament is so minimal that he does not even want to read and study it. Anyway, it is good that these facts are not known and that those examinations usually don't go too deeply into the Old Testament.[42]

His mother showed her concern in a letter addressed to her son Walter. His answer appears to be indicative of his lifelong independent spirit:

> Dear Mother, I have known it for a long time that it would be more profitable for me to hold the same beliefs as others. But Christ says, "I have been born and have come into the world in order to give witness to the truth"—that is, the truth and not the beliefs held by the pharisees. For this He paid with his life. And He also says, "He who is of the truth, hears my voice."
> It is for me to ask, "what is the gospel of Jesus Christ?" and not, "what is the gospel of the people around me?" I have to believe what is *true*, and not what is held to be true by a certain class of people. When you say, "stop worrying, believe in the entire Word!"—the same words came to all the men who have brought us the purer truth we possess and who had to struggle for it. If they had heeded this admonition, we would all today still be Catholics. They would have had a pleasant life and would have lost their souls. "To believe in the entire Word?" I have no desire more serious than to perceive and to believe in the whole truth of Jesus Christ and the entire Word of God. But where do I find this entire Word? In the attitudes of the German Baptist preachers? If this be true then we would have done no more than to exchange the infallible Roman Church for the infallible Baptist Church. I don't know who could give me the guarantee that I was not turning my back at Jesus Christ and His teachings if I accepted, contrary to the urgings of my heart, the religious beliefs of this particular group.
> You will consider it conceit when I say that I know better than a large number of men who are all older etc. than I am. It is daring what I am doing, but I cannot do otherwise. As long as I believe that the voice of God and the word of God in the New Testament and also in the Old Testament are on my side, I must stand by it, even though I may stand alone—but, thank God, I don't stand alone.
> This is all the consolation I am able to offer to you: I believe in the gospel of Jesus Christ, with all my heart. What this gospel is, everyone has to decide for himself, in the face of his God. I am now stepping into father's and your footsteps. When you left the great and old Lutheran Church in order to join the small and ill-renowned Baptist Church, you too invoked the right to interpret the Scriptures according to your own conscience; now, I am doing the same.
> I am looking forward to the council undisturbed. Whatever its decision may be, I will be satisfied.[43]

The council then did show itself satisfied and it recommended ordination, which was carried out on October 21.[44]

After the ordination his mother moved in with him, in New York, and kept house for him. From the very beginning, his parents' marriage had been under an ill star. It is possible that his father was unable ever to forget his first love.[45] Even in his childhood, Walter had been exposed to his parents' quarrels.[46] It seems that the rift between the parents also separated the children from each other, and Walter turned to his mother.[47] Among other things, August Rauschenbusch reproached his wife for her lack of piety and maintained that Walter had inherited this trait from her. He was very satisfied with the separation.[48] It is easy to see that the relationship between father and son was not ideal under these circumstances. Often the father criticized the son,[49] and nowhere are there indications that the son would have been essentially influenced in theological matters by his father. For instance, when Walter Rauschenbusch began to be interested in the social attitudes of the Baptists and the Mennonites, he turned to his trusted, respected friend and teacher of ecclesiastical history, Benjamin O. True, who seems to be the first to point out to him that August Rauschenbusch was one of the first and leading researchers on the Mennonites in America.[50]

It is certain that there are many similarities between father and son and that both had lasting influences, each in his field. However, it is important to see Walter Rauschenbusch's independent stand. It would be difficult to speak of an "eminent father-son teaching team" in this case.[51] After Walter's ordination he definitely decided to stay in New York. When his mother went to live with him in his rented apartment, the family broke apart and Walter communicated with his father only through friends.[52]

### The Quest for a Theological Footing

After these many crises and uncertainties had been resolved, Rauschenbusch was able to devote all his attention to pastoral work. In retrospect he sums up this period in one of the images typical of his way of thinking: "After my last letter to you I have had many experiences. It often seems to me that I am living very fast. Yes, if iron is to become steel, it has to go from heat to cold and back again. . . . My work is making very encouraging progress and I feel very satisfied with it."[53]

On November 21, 1886 he carried out baptism for the first time, baptizing five people.[54] He felt that the members of his congregation were fond of him and that more and more people were coming under his influence. He established a Sunday school class in the morning before the church worship service. In it he quite freely discussed "all kinds of practical, ethical and religious questions."[55] Stimulated by an article in

*Der Sendbote*, he wrote his first contribution to this paper entitled "The Washing of Feet." In this article he warned that ritual washing of the feet alone, such as that of the Pope or of the Austrian emperor, carried within itself the danger of overlooking the real responsibilities of neighborly duties. Our relationship with our invisible Lord requires

> a repeated, visible, symbolic representation. Our relationship with our visible, ever-present neighbors does not require such a representation. Symbolic expression of loving service cannot further the practical application of such love; it only increases the danger that we become satisfied with the beautiful symbol and forget the unpleasant task itself.[56]

He tried to write especially for young people. At this time he was only 25 years of age and felt very much like one of them. He exhorted them to take part regularly in the youth meetings.[57] In vain would one look for signs of his deviant theological beliefs in all these activities. He apparently knew how to conceal them. Later he remembered that "my idea then was to save souls in the ordinarily accepted religious sense."[58] His short articles give proof of this fact. He did not have a fully worked-through theological position. The truth is that in the extant parts of his correspondence there can be found indications of his need to find a solid basis through theological discussions.

He seems to have conducted such discussions especially with two old friends of his who were also on their way to pastoral service. One of these was Edward Hanna, his friend since they both had attended the Free Academy in Rochester,[59] and who had studied at the Propaganda in Rome and become resident professor at the American College in Rome.[60] The other one was Ernst Cremer, his friend since the time when they both had been at the *gymnasium* in Gütersloh in Germany. Cremer was at the time preparing for his examinations.[61] Only the letters by these two friends have been preserved. They do not seem to have been of much help to Rauschenbusch since neither of these friends at the time had a theological standpoint of his own. But these letters are proof of the fact that Rauschenbusch was seeking such a basis.

## An Insight into Social Inequity

In this situation he was open to the peculiar form of socialism advocated by Henry George through his idea of the single tax. Rauschenbusch later admitted "I owe my own first awakening to the world of social problems to the agitation of Henry George in 1886, and I wish here to record my life-long debt to this single-minded apostle of a great truth." [62] In 1886 Henry George was a candidate for mayor of New York City, but it seems that the election campaign itself and the ideas propagated in it did not influence Rauschenbusch; he did not remark on it. If there was any influence, it could have shown up only later.[63]

Henry George received his strongest support from religious circles through Edward McGlynn, an Irish-American priest in the largest and most popular Catholic community of New York, St. Stephen's. He attracted with equal power the working people and the religious community of New York. After his defeat in the mayoral election, Henry George really started to put his ideas into practice, especially by establishing the "Anti-Poverty-Society." Rauschenbusch reports:

> I remember how Father McGlynn, speaking at Cooper Union in the first Single Tax campaign in New York, in 1886, recited the words, "Thy kingdom come! Thy will be done on earth," and as the great audience realized for the first time the social significance of the holy words, it lifted them off their seats with a shout of joy.[64]

Very probably he describes his own experience in these words. But McGlynn did not make this speech, known under the title "The Cross of the New Crusade," in 1886 but rather for the first time on March 29, 1887.[65] And he repeated it several times thereafter. Henry George reported on this same event in the following way:

> Never before in New York had a great audience sprung to its feet and in a tumult of enthusiasm cheered the Lord's Prayer; but it is the Lord's Prayer with a meaning that the churches have ignored. These simple words, "Thy kingdom come, Thy will be done *on earth* as it is in Heaven," as they fall from the lips of a Christian priest who proclaimed the common Fatherhood of God and the common Brotherhood of men; who points to the widespread poverty and suffering not as in accordance with God's will but in defiance of God's order, and who appeals to the love of God and the hope of heaven, not to make men submissive to social injustice, which brings want and misery to man but instead to urge them to the duty of sweeping away this injustice— [these words] have in them the power with which Christianity conquered the world.[66]

If from the above we get the impression that this event was the decisive stimulus for Rauschenbusch to begin to walk the road which led him to the social gospel, then this impression is even deepened when we read a letter he sent to Germany only two weeks following this experience. In this letter he mentions for the first time his interest in social conditions:

> In the past year I have grown much older. I want to say more experienced, not more exhausted.
> The circle of my active life has very much widened and with it also the sphere of my sympathies. Ever since I came to New York I have done very little reading of books but a lot of living with people; I found out what makes them tick, what they think about, what they are striving for. Much of what I used to find appealing in novels and in poetry seems untrue and artificial to me now. There is much too much real misery in the world for people to be brooding over invented pain.

> There are two things which at present occupy my main interest and dominate my thinking. One thing of concern are the present social conditions, the unequal distribution of property and the growing and justified tension between those who have and those who don't have. Here in New York the gap between the two is very great. The other thing is the spiritual needs of the people around me. I believe that man is more than a superior kind of swine and that his situation is not very much improved by more food, by a better position, etc., such as is the case with an animal. My real question is, how a man can really be made better, what it is that has power over his soul so that his main question would not be, "What is pleasurable?" but rather, "What is right?" Maybe this seems to you to be a narrow description of my task, but if I had a complete solution of this question, I would be far ahead of many another who uses much bigger words and yet does not know what he really wants.[67]

Thus we see that to Rauschenbusch, the preacher, and to Rauschenbusch, the church historian, now is added Rauschenbusch, the emerging social reformer.

Rauschenbusch's sermons from this period have been thoroughly examined by Max L. Stackhouse. He finds that the tone of the sermons remains quite conservative up to 1891, in spite of the fact that Rauschenbausch's thinking becomes increasingly radicalized. However, he finds certain theological transformations in them.[68] In the spring of 1887 Rauschenbusch began to discuss the problem of faith and grace. He abandoned the concept of faith as being equal to "considering as true," and he now saw faith as being the confidence in future possibilities.[69] In the fall of that year he progressed to the stage when his first sermon, entitled "Why believe?" appeared in print.[70] Based on his own experiences, his definition of "faith" was that it is comparable to the confidence in a physician who, with trembling hands, is performing surgery on the eye:

> Faith is the confidence one person has in another. Such confidence is then manifested, among other things, in that one believes the words spoken and the promises given by that person. Faith in God is exactly like that.[71]

Contrary to faith is an attitude which strives for riches and reputation, because this requires a man's entire strength and also his use of force. In such a situation it becomes very difficult to observe truth and honesty, neighborly love and charity.[72] In an article published in *Der Sendbote* in January 1888, he phrased his ideas by saying that faith was "a quiet, confident holding on. When all is dark, when practical reason cannot find a way out, when even the deepest knowledge can no longer feel any ground under its feet, it is then that the clear and quiet voice of faith is heard."[73]

This is the first time that a definable movement became evident. After having pondered a problem for some time, Rauschenbusch then brought it out into the open, for discussion, usually as an article in *Der Sendbote* or in other journals. Later his articles were generally published in the magazine *For the Right*, of which he was co-editor.

Speaking of the progress he was making in clarifying his social interests, we may say that during this period he was still gathering information. During his vacation he visited a state prison for juvenile offenders and was deeply impressed. He spent the last days of his vacation at the seashore because he wanted to see how people lived in a resort place.[74] He needed such experiences in order to prepare his sermons properly. These experiences were more valuable to him than commentaries and theological works:

> All such stuff does not help me very much. If I have the basic text of the Bible and people in the original, I mostly don't need to worry about my material.[75]

From such expreriences he derived a clear knowledge of the extent of social problems. In 1888 he began to describe such experiences in short articles. Sharpe gives a detailed account of the second one of these articles, entitled "Beneath the Glitter." In that paper Rauschenbusch described the radical difference between the shiny façade of the metropolis of New York and the misery of the poor people whose exploitation made all the glitter possible. He said, "Guess I am something of a crank on these things. Wish you'd trot around with me for a week; you wouldn't think so highly of things as they are."[76]

An article published earlier, under the title "The Saving Efficacy of Money," was based on Jesus' saying that it is more difficult for a rich man to save his soul than it is for a camel to go through a needle's eye. In the religious life, however, Rauschenbusch said that it is a fact that a rich man has more possibilities to assure his salvation than does a poor man. Thus, the most beautiful and most comfortable churches are to be found in the wealthiest districts of the cities. It is true that they also have concern for the poor, but only to an extent which could be compared to the grape harvest when some grapes are left on the vines ... for the poor. This was in accordance with Jesus' pronouncement, contrary to common practice, that the rich had to overcome greater difficulties on their way to the Kingdom.[77]

Toward the end of 1887, Rauschenbusch prepared a manuscript on Henry George. It seems that he had been preoccupied with this topic during the entire year. On the last manuscript page is the remark, "My first paper on the social question."[78] The paper concludes with these observations:

> Dear friends, there is a social question. No one can doubt it, in whose ears are ringing the wailings of the mangled and the crushed, who are borne along on the pent-up torrent of human life. Woe to the man who stands afar off and says: Peace, peace, when there is no peace. The Jews were blinded by existing customs and the traditions of their fathers, and they rejected Christ. Let us take heed lest we too bow to that which is, and refuse allegiance to that which *ought to be*.[79]

Apart from his renewed interest in social questions, he still remained faithful to his first love, church history. On December 19 he read a paper on the Waldensians at one of the regular meetings of Baptist ministers of New York.[80] Medieval history for him had a compelling and lasting interest.[81] But in his historical writings as well as in his sermons of that period, there is little indication of his recently developed social concerns.

With all the above, Walter Rauschenbusch's wide range of interests was by no means exhausted. As the deeply concerned man that he was, he had many different interests and was exposed to many different influences. Some of his other activities were, for instance, his lifelong support of missions.[82] He kept in close contact with his missionary sister Emma and her influence must be taken into account. Because of his position and because he had a perfect command of English as well as German, he was an ideal representative of immigrant congregations. He was often asked to speak on topics related to immigrants, and that at a time when many people were recommending changes in the immigration policy as a means of improving social conditions.

Rauschenbusch also had a lifelong quiet love of poetry. This was part of a family tradition. His sister Emma too wrote poetry.[83] While Walter wrote poems infrequently,[84] he also used his talent to translate devotional songs into German and later to write his famous prayers.[85] He considered songs an essential means of awakening social consciousness.[86]

## The Christianity of Social Work

While his many interests were all somewhat related, the social question appeared to assume more and more importance in his edifice of thought:

> I began to work in New York and there among the working people my social education began. I began to understand the connection between religious and social questions. I had no social outlook before. I hadn't known how society could be saved. When I had begun to apply my previous religious ideas to the conditions I found, I discovered that they didn't fit.
>
> All this time my friends were urging me to give up this social work and devote myself to "Christian work." Some of them felt grieved for me, but I knew the work was Christ's work and I went ahead, although I had to set myself against all that I had previously been taught. I had to go back to the Bible to find out whether I or my friends were right. I had to revise my whole study of the Bible. Then I began to write for newspapers. That is where my ideas began to clear up.
>
> People didn't want to hear my message; they had no mind for it; they would take all I said about religion in the way they had been used to it, but they didn't want any of "this social stuff." All my scientific study of the Bible was undertaken to find a basis for the Christian teaching of a social gospel.[87]

His biblical studies, of which he speaks above, were begun at the end of 1887 and at the beginning of 1888, with an exegesis of First Corinthians 12. In this epistle he found a biblical basis for his concept of the church as a social organism:

> A congregation is a community freely established by number of people with the aim of furthering the Kingdom of God within themselves and in others. These people are brought together by this common purpose, and not because of equality of education, wealth or occupation. This is why there is found a great variety of natural talents and of experiences in a congregation.
> A congregation is a wonderful organism which is able to activate its life-force in a hundred different directions, and in every new direction new gifts are displayed.[88]

This notion of the church as being an organism becomes an essential component of Rauschenbusch's theological system. It is mainly based on the exegesis of the New Testament, although it very likely also incorporated new social theories from Germany and England and was influenced by the spread of evolutionary theories.

Still more interesting is an article by Rauschenbusch on the commandment "Thou Shalt not Steal." In this article he expresses his fundamental ideas on trade, on property, and on the causes of the unequal distribution of wealth. He states that, originally, man's natural environment is God's gift to man. But this does not preclude the right to personal ownership:

> Something becomes our property when we use the raw material offered by God through his creation and when we direct the forces of nature so that they satisfy our wishes.
> This right to ownership we may also extend to others. . . . Equitable trade always means that each party receives something which has at least the same value for him as that which he gives up. . . .
> We speak of theft when a person takes property away from another without giving him in return something which for him has the same or a greater value than that which was taken from him. If, therefore, it is a question of someone acquiring property without giving something of equivalent value in return, we may say with some assurance that, consciously or unconsciously, dishonesty is at work. If, for example, someone buys stock at the stock exchange and pays $10,000 for it and then, through some manipulations, he sells the stock the next day with a $1,000 profit, then we ask where the $1,000 had come from. Has he carried out any work which was worth $1,000? . . . Certainly not. . . . I believe that such money is not earned and that it is, therefore, dishonest profit. . . .
> This is why Paul says, "He who does not work, shall not eat." Because if someone does not work and yet he eats, then he is eating bread which was earned by someone else's sweat.[89]

This radical attitude hits hard at the foundations of the capitalist economic system. Rauschenbusch desired to make as direct and clear an application of the gospel as was possible; thus he sought to make "the Gospel simple so that slow-working brains may understand it."[90]

Another article related to these ideas is part of a collection of sermons on the four Gospel writers, published in *Der Sendbote* in the fall 1888.[91] There he writes, speaking of Luke.

> He was full of charity toward the poor and the abandoned. We see this expressed in his writings. He is the only one who tells the parable of the rich man and that of Lazarus, and that of the feast when the Lord commanded that the poor, the cripples and the lame be brought in. He is the only one who reports what the Savior says at the very beginning of His active life, namely, that the Lord had sent him to preach the Gospel to the poor, and also how Jesus tells John the Baptist that it is an indication of His Kingdom when the Gospel is being preached to the poor. The Gospel according to Luke is particularly addressed to the poor and the lost. He is the only one who tells of the great sinner, the woman; of the prodigal son; of Zacchaeus, of the acceptance of the repentent criminal on the cross; of the Lord's prayer for his executioners. And it is Luke alone who has preserved for us the words of Jesus, saying "There will be more joy in heaven over one repentant sinner than over ninety-nine just who do not need to repent."

## BROTHERHOOD OF THE KINGDOM

It had now become evident that, at least from December 1887 on, Rauschenbusch sought to work out a position large enough to embrace all of his interests. But he was not alone in this endeavor. In the spring of 1888, but possibly even earlier, he struck up a friendship with Leighton Williams and Nathaniel Schmidt. Williams was pastor of the close-by Amity Baptist Church, Schmidt was pastor of a Swedish Baptist Church.[92] These three friends constituted the germinal group for the Brotherhood of the Kingdom which was established in 1892.[93] Thus, Rauschenbusch could focus on a special task and he had friends with whom he was able to discuss the new ideas.

He liked his work with his congregation:

> So far my activities here are all progressing. I like my work. I try to be as popular and interesting in my sermons as I can be. It does not happen often that my listeners would not give me their undivided attention.[94]

At this point Walter received a call to become, like his father, a professor at the seminary in Rochester. His father intended to retire. Previously, Walter had made it clear that he did not feel any inclination in that direction. In spite of this, the council unanimously offered the appointment to him and seriously pleaded with him to accept it. He declined. First he gave reasons of bad health, but he added:

> In the last few weeks, another reason has emerged more and more strongly. I am hesitant to give up my life as a preacher and pastor so soon, in order to spend my life in the hothouse atmosphere of a learned institution. I still need the contact with the

> people, simple work modeled after my Master's, if my own inner life is to go on growing. This is why I would prefer to continue working here for another while. It seems to me that my work here has not yet been completed.⁹⁵

A year later the position at the Seminary had not yet been filled. Augustus H. Strong, president of the Seminary, again asked him to reconsider his decision. But Rauschenbusch's answer was the same as before.⁹⁶ It was not until 1897 that he felt "complete joy" in accepting a renewed offer.⁹⁷

In the winter of 1888, writes Sharpe, Rauschenbusch became ill with a cold. "In order to answer the call of suffering mankind"⁹⁸ he got up too soon, and suffered a relapse which further impaired his hearing. On March 12, New York experienced the most severe storm in a long time. Of the two hundred casualties, 24 persons died in the streets of the city.⁹⁹ While his loss of hearing cannot be ascribed to these circumstances alone, he nevertheless began to feel that the suffering caused by his loss of hearing made his work increasingly burdensome. At the end of that year, he reported that he had also lost considerable weight and:

> My full beard has grown to be a permanent institution of this land, because I do not want to become a martyr of the barbershop like a modern . . . what was the name of the mythological character whose liver was being eaten away by the vultures?¹⁰⁰

## Toward Point of No Return

In 1888, Rauschenbusch attended two conferences. We are inclined to say that one was geared to the piety of the preacher, the other to the training of the social reformer. The first was one of Moody's Northfield Meetings, the other the Baptist Congress. Regarding the first he wrote as follows:

> Indeed, life is wonderfully sweet here. It is a near approach to heaven. The green leaves and the faraway beauty of the Connecticut Valley; the ramble through the glens and fields with saintly souls; the lift and rush of the spirit in the great meetings; the absence of wickedness and the simplicity and trustfulness of intercourse and the constant turning of thoughts on God's truth and Christ's love; surely heaven cannot be very unlike all this. . . .
> Two things are fundamental to the thinking of this Conference: the authority of the Bible and the reality of the direct work of God's spirit on the spirit of man.¹⁰¹

At the Baptist Congress, in December, he delivered an address on the topic, "Who Shall Educate? Church or State?" He observed that education was coming more and more under control of the state. He agreed with this trend because it was in keeping with increasing democratization:

> I find throughout the governments of the nations that there is a drifting away from monarchical government to democratic. I believe that tendency is of God, and that a

government of the people, and by the people, is the divine ideal towards which we ought to stretch forward.[102]

As responsibilities for human welfare have increasingly come under the control of the state, so education should also, because all of these responsibilities concern society as a whole:

> One by one, the laws of the Kingdom of Heaven are becoming the laws of the kingdoms of this earth. The Church is ever pressing onward and the State is following on. Where the Church once stood, the State now stands. Where the Church now stands, the State will stand in the future.[103]

In saying this, Rauschenbusch stated for the first time his idea of the Christianization of the social order. Another speaker at the same Congress expressed similar thoughts. He said:

> There are always new fields of beneficence open and the Church can always stay far in advance of the State, till the day comes when all society is reached by the leaven of Christianity, the State is absorbed into the Church, and the Kingdom of Christ is realized on earth.[104]

In the fall, 1888, the idea of the Kingdom of God here on earth was already alive among Rauschenbusch's friends. Williams had read a paper entitled "The Established Tendencies Toward Social Reform" at the New York Baptist Pastor's Conference; he also had it published. Rauschenbusch reviewed this article in the press. His description of Williams could just as well be a description of himself:

> The author of this pamphlet is one of that growing class of young men who, aroused by what they see about them and constrained by the Spirit of Christ within them, are giving some of their most earnest thought to social questions. He is not one of those who believe that the world is quite as good as can be desired, and that anyone who fails to get along must be either lazy, intemperate or unlucky. He sees a great pushing and striving for a better life and a more universal happiness. That striving is only the old millenial hope for the Kingdom of God on earth. The realization of it is made constantly more urgent by the increasing strain of our new industrial life, which demands new adjustments. Political economy is giving precision and direction to the vague demands that are stirring the masses of people everywhere.[105]

In retrospect, it becomes clear that, starting in December, 1887, or in 1888, Rauschenbusch was giving much thought to, and becoming deeply involved in the social question.

In order to avoid the impression that these were the only problems which concerned him, we must point out his other activities as well. On October 27, 1887, he delivered a speech on "The Importance of the Proper Christian Education of Our German Population" at the New York Baptist Preachers Meeting. At least from that time on he appeared to be an acknowledged leader of the immigrant churches. He had always maintained that it was necessary for the dissemination of the gospel to preach to the immigrants in their native tongues. Although in his own congregation he gradually substituted English for the German language, [106] he defended and justified the existence of foreign-language congregations in America. He pointed out the statistics showing relatively more successful results of these churches.[107] He also supported the continuation of a liberal immigration policy, partly justifying it in a rather surprising way:

> I think this very pressure of the population brought on by immigration is a boon to us; even the anarchists are a boon to us, for the explosion of a dynamite bomb has set us thinking. We have been turning our attention to social questions in a way we have never done before.[108]

His justification was obviously a superficial one forcing him further to analyze the relationship of social reform and the use of force.

When he became a member of the Telugu Committee of the Baptist Missionary Union, his interest in missionary activities increased. He presented the report of the Committee at the meeting in Boston of the Union in May, 1889.[109] In *Der Sendbote* we also find a few short articles on topics concerning missions [110] and, from 1888 on, he was Secretary for the Affairs of the Missions at the Eastern Conference of German Baptists.[111]

After 1888, Rauschenbusch focused his studies on the New Testament and sociology, somewhat to the neglect of church history. This course seemed more profitable to him.[112] And it did prove to be more profitable as a preparation for future discussions of the social question.

## Is Force Justified?

In his thinking, he had to answer the question of what means should be employed in the modification of social conditions. Is the use of force permissible if it brings about very rapid improvements? On March 27 his article appeared in *Der Sendbote*, entitled "To Hit or To Endure?" in which he decisively stated his relationship to radical socialism:

> We are continually colliding with other people who are all engaged in constant running and shoving; if one doesn't, like Robinson Crusoe, live on an isolated island, one gets stepped upon all the time. Our interests are at logger-heads. To hit or to endure?—usually one or the other has to be chosen. . . . In other words, if we are taken advantage of, should we quietly endure it or should we take revenge?

He then goes back to Christ's commandment which says that we should not repay evil with evil but with good. And he cites Paul when he says that revenge is not ours but God's alone. It is even better to suffer a wrong than to begin an argument. Jesus himself gave the best example:

If it ever was justified to protest a wrong and to forcibly defend oneself against it, then it was the moment when Christ was arrested in order to be murdered. One of the apostles tried to do just that, and Jesus reprimanded him. And standing before Pilate, He said that it was characteristic of His Kingdom—which was not of this earth—that its citizens did not practice forceful resistance.

Even after having discussed and analyzed a number of possible counter arguments, he still maintained that it is possible to lead a pacifist life. Although some arguments are justifiable, such as that of punishment as a deterrent and with the purpose of protecting society, it still is the role of the Christian to follow the example given by Christ. Answering a wrong with the use of force can only create another wrong.

> If we endure a wrong, only one wrong has been committed. If we defend ourselves, we can be sure that a second and a third wrong will be committed. . . . It is a generally accepted idea that the use of force always harms the one who is exercising it. . . . It is not even so difficult to obey this commandment. All in all we would go through life more easily and more happily than most of us do now. But this is not the highest motivation for such behavior. The truly highest motivation is simply the fact that it is right. And if something is right, it is also wise and useful.

Yet, all around there existed unjust conditions, especially in the big city of New York:

> Any system of land tenure which enables man to hold land idle in the midst of great cities, where dying children and weary women moan for more space, is unjust and ought to be changed.[113]

Such injustices make an ethical life well-nigh impossible.[114] Nevertheless, any forcible change would not be an acceptable solution.[115]

Stackhouse tells us that Rauschenbusch preached his first complete sermon on a social question in the spring of 1889. In that sermon he maintained that it is the role of the United States in the world to give witness to liberty, democracy, and social equality. Only enlightened and just people can uphold a free nation. It is the special role of the Baptists to be a model of pure democracy.[116]

## Hiatus

During the next few months, Rauschenbusch had little time for further articles on topical questions. Until October, 1889, he had to give all of his attention to his congregation. But he did write a defense of Bellamy's *Looking Backward, 2000-1887*, and of the movement connected with it.[117] Rauschenbusch was truly impressed by Bellamy's work.

In the past three years, his congregation had grown from 143 to 213 members.[118] The church building had become too small, especially for the evening meetings.[119] Plans for an extension of the building were soon abandoned and, instead, the building was sold for $29,000. This amount was sufficient for the purchase of a lot in a quieter district, on 45th Street near Tenth Avenue. Construction of the new building was estimated at $24,000. This meant that Rauschenbusch had to devise ways of financing the project. He began to write Sunday School lessons which he submitted to *The Christian Inquirer*. He used the money to help with the financial obligations of his congregation.[120]

Since his seminary days, he had been a friend of Charles Strong, the son of Augustus H. Strong.[121] An old friendship between Augustus Strong and John D. Rockefeller, a Baptist, brought Charles Strong to visit the Rockefellers quite frequently. The affectionate relationship of Charles Strong and Bessie Rockefeller, the oldest daughter, led to their marriage in April, 1889.[122] Rauschenbusch was invited to the marriage ceremony and he presented the young couple with a collection of prints by the German artist Heinrich Hoffmann, depicting scenes from the life of Christ.[123]

It is possible that it was these circumstances that encouraged Rauschenbusch to ask Rockefeller for help. In his usual manner, Rockefeller first made inquiries at the Baptist City Mission. Then he promised a donation in the amount of $8,000, with the condition that the congregation would provide the remaining $16,000 before March, 1890.[124] At the time of the dedication of the new building, the City Mission had agreed to contribute an additional $8,000. The remaining $11,000 of the final cost of $27,000 was covered by the congregation.[125] The foundation stone was laid on October 19, 1889,[126] and in April, 1890, it was possible for the dedication ceremonies to take place.

The new building was a simple one. It was three stories high, and had many airy rooms for the various and still-expanding activities of the congregation.[127] Rauschenbusch had been fully occupied with the necessary negotiations: "It was a lot of trouble. I can tell you now much more easily what the cost of a hundred bricks is than I would be able to conjugate Greek verbs."[128]

At the end of September, Rauschenbusch took part in the Federal Conference of German Baptists in Milwaukee. He was elected a member of the Seminary Committee.[129] During his stay in Milwaukee he met, for the first time, Pauline Rother, who was to become his wife in 1893.[130]

## For the Right

The fall of that year was to be a rather dramatic period for Rauschenbusch and Williams. In October, the first issue of *For the Right* was published.[131] Since that magazine has been described in detail by both Sharpe and Bodein, only some pertinent facts will be given here. Apart from Rauschenbusch and Williams, editorship was held also by Elizabeth Post and J. E. Raymond. The magazine had a Christian-social orientation. It was published mainly in order to represent the interests of the working people of New York City. It has been argued, possibly rightly so, that the magazine, because of its form and its subject matter, had no chance of fullfilling its alleged purpose.[132] Also, it was the only attempt to address those who were supposed to initiate social reforms and who should have benefited most by them. Nevertheless, it was a serious attempt by the editors to put into practice their ideas on social reform.

Both friends exhibited the same seriousness of purpose at the Baptist Congress in November, 1889.[133] Williams was Congress secretary. When the discussion turned to Henry George and the Single Tax, Rauschenbusch and Williams received permission to take the rostrum. Rauschenbusch used this opportunity to present his recently formulated attitude on the responsibilities of the church:

> It is certainly true that it is one of the main objects of Christianity to change the individual life, and to implant in the heart of man the truth and love of the Lord Jesus Christ. But I claim that that is only one-half of the object of Christianity, that the other half is to bring in the Kingdom of God, and that the efforts of the Christian Church ought to be directed in a like measure to the accomplishment of that last object, and that not only indirectly by changing the individual and gradually having the influence emanate from him but directly, and then having the influence of society re-act upon the individual.[134]

What must the church do in order to make the Kingdom of God a reality?

> We must . . . attack the wrongs of human society and the unjust laws of the community to bring about righteousness through the Kingdom of God in the world, and then we shall also have an influence radiating from society and centering upon the individual.[135]

In this respect, Rauschenbusch was at least able to agree with George on the means necessary to improve the social situation: He mentioned unfair customs policies and land speculation as typical examples of unjust conditions. He recommended modifications of customs practices which create artificial monopolies and nationalization of industries which have a natural monopoly, such as the transportation industry. But he indicated that Henry George did not go far enough:

> There is where the socialists and Mr. George disagree. He says that after *laissez-faire* has been secured, social ills would stop and go no further. The socialists say that even after that we should still have many of the phenomena of social life that at present distress us; and I, for my part, cannot but think that they are right. Even after that, there would still be a power of the stronger over the weaker.[136]

## CHRISTIANITY'S TWO FOCAL POINTS

Not many of the participants of the Baptist Congress could or would go all the way with Williams and Rauschenbusch, for they belong to the extreme left wing of this already quite liberal Baptist convention. The discussion of the relationship of church and state which followed gave Rauschenbusch an opportunity to clarify the theological background of his views. At the beginning of the convention, the traditionally Baptist dogma of the radical separation of church and state had been presented. This presentation provided some exciting ideas for Rauschenbusch, and he offered a view of his own:

> I read a short time ago the life of that great and noble man, Thomas Arnold of Rugby, and also that of Frederick Dennison Maurice: and I remember that they held the view that the Church and State are necessarily, and in their nature, one. . . . The State must be built on righteousness. Its very purpose is to exercise righteousness among men, and its ultimate goal is to be merged in the Kingdom of God which is to come on earth. The kingdoms of this world shall become the kingdoms of the Christ, and the day shall come when every knee shall bow and every tongue shall confess that Jesus Christ is Lord to the glory of God the Father. That is the ultimate glorious ideal towards which the whole organization of the world must be tending. That is the ideal of the State. Now what has the Church to do with it? . . . I believe in the prophetic ministry of the Christian Church within the State. I believe that the Church is composed of men who are touched with the power of the life to come, with the power of the *aion mellon*, of the world era that is coming. They see, the things that shall be in the future, but which are not yet. The Church must announce those things in the ears of the State; it must declare that truth which is not yet recognized. . . . We must be [Christians and citizens] at the same time, and we can be that in just one way—by being animated by the life of Jesus Christ, and by carrying that life into the State in every direction.[137]

We get the impression that this statement already expresses the essential points of Rauschenbusch's social gospel. Later he revised it but did not really modify it. Basically, he is saying the following: Christianity has two focal points, the salvation of the individual and the creation of a just society. The perfection of the social order and the perfection of the church go hand in hand. They constitute the Kingdom of God. The most appropriate way of social transformation is socialism.

Rauschenbusch got acquainted with Maurice as early as 1886. Undoubtedly, this man's ideas strongly influenced Rauschenbusch's social philosophy. It can safely be assumed that Rauschenbusch's friendship with Williams deepened this influence. While Rauschenbusch had been educated in part in Germany, Williams was oriented toward England. Since the 1880's, he visited England once every ten years.[138] Maurice had fearlessly used the expression Christian socialism, and this fact probably encouraged Rauschenbusch to do the same.

It will have to be said, nevertheless, that Rauschenbusch misunderstood Maurice. Maurice had, in fact, always been misunderstood, even by his friends who had collaborated with him during the first short phase of a Christian socialism. At the end of that period, on September 24, 1852, Maurice wrote the following to his closest collaborator, J. M. Ludlow:

> My business, because I am a theologian, and have no vocation except for theology, is not to build but to dig, to show that economy and politics must have a ground beneath themselves; that society is not to be made anew by arrangements of ours, but it is to be regenerated by finding the law and ground of its order and harmony, the only secret is its existence in God. This must seem to you an unpractical and unchristian method; to me it's the only one that makes action possible, and Christianity anything more than an artificial religion for the use of believers. . . . The Kingdom of Heaven is to me the great practical existing reality which is to renew the earth and make it a habitation for blessed spirits instead of for demons.
> To preach the Gospel of that Kingdom, the fact that it is among us, and is not to be set up at all, is my calling and business. . . .
> But if ever I do any good work, and earn any of the hatred, which the godly in Christ Jesus receive, and have a right to, it must be in the way I have indicated, by proclaiming society and humanity to be divine realities, *as they stand*, not as they may become, and by calling upon the priests, kings, prophets of the world to answer for their sin in having made them unreal by separating them from the living and eternal God who has established them in Christ for His glory. This is what I call digging, this is what I oppose to building.[139]

Maurice rejected all attempts at being made into a reformer.[140] But Rauschenbusch was so persuaded in the idea of evolution and also was too activist to forsake the need to contribute to social progress himself. To him, human misery, caused by industrialization, was so oppressive that he could not remain inactive. Among the progressive men of his time, he was an "impatient liberal."[141]

In the following year, 1890, Rauschenbusch did not take part in the Baptist Congress; and in 1891 he was in Germany, so that he did not again appear at that forum until 1892.

Until his departure for Germany, he continued writing his Sunday-school lessons, his contributions to *For the Right* and several articles for *Der Sendbote*. In his contributions to *For the Right* he was able to develop his ideas on the practical realization of a better social order. His articles published in *Der Sendbote*, however, gave him the opportunity to discuss the theological importance of the social question with the members of his own church. These facts constitute the significance of his writings at that time.

In June, 1890, E. Anschütz, one of the older preachers, published an article entitled "The Social Question."[142] Therein he said: "For a considerable period of time we will not be able to avoid grappling with this burning problem of our times . . . and that also because Holy Scripture itself gives us an answer, namely, the answer to the 'social question.'" He saw the causes of the related problems mainly in moral deficiencies on the part of the dissatisfied lower classes: First, they are more sensitive; there has always been poverty, but in recent times man has become more sensitive in regard to it. Second, greed, that is, the need to participate in all the luxuries, "People go beyond their means, misery comes in, and people complain about conditions which could have been avoided through wise use of their means." Third, the awakening feeling of independence in man. The old relationships of dependence are no longer accepted. This, too, leads to moral deficiency, "The attitude now is to take advantage of the other person rather than granting him an advantage."

Anschütz saw the causes of problematic issues as inherent in character deficiencies of those who are dissatisfied, rather than in deficiencies inherent in social conditions. This is also the basis for his criticism of the main arguments held by the defenders of the "social question": First, their ideology is materialistic, earthbound, and therefore contradicts Christianity. An attitude which tries to abolish evil by changing social circumstances denies the reality of sin. Second, the abolishment of class differences can only lead to a right based on the use of force, to a war of all against all. It is wrong to demand the abolition of the class structure instead of demanding reconciliation among the social classes. Third, nationalization of industries is a totally wrong approach to the problem.

> It is not the outward circumstances which need to be reformed; it is the proper attitude which needs to be created. The "social question" wants to be solved from the inside out, through proper understanding.

Here it becomes obvious that the problems in question are, in reality, questions put to the church:

> The state may, indeed, have a role in the solution of the "social question," namely, to regulate the material conditions. We do not wish to deny that. But the main task is and remains to be a task of the religious community. It is this community which has to create the right attitude. . . . In proportion to the extent to which the Gospel finds its way into the hearts of men and that the great social ideas presented by Jesus are accepted and realized, to that extent will the social question be solved. The great social idea of the Gospel, however, is: "Love thy neighbor as thyself." The "social question" can be solved only through very thorough preparatory work done by the community.

The entire article is an authoritative presentation of the attitudes held by the German Baptists in America, as well as by others, in regard to the social problems of that time.[143]

## RAUSCHENBUSCH AND ACTIVISM

Previously Rauschenbusch had not reacted to similar statements appearing in *Der Sendbote*.[144] He did not even answer a quite violent attack on McGlynn [145] whom he highly respected. Rauschenbusch also refused to write an article of this nature when he was asked, in the summer 1889, by the editor of *Der Sendbote* to do so.[146] But by now Rauschenbusch had grown into something like an activist—as was pointed out above—and he felt himself sufficiently prepared to enter into a discussion.

When he finally did so, very cautiously, he did not present all of his thoughts but rather began by agreeing with the author of the first article mentioned above:

> So far we, as congregations, have distinguished ourselves mainly by keeping silent in regard to the social question. We have generally used the excuse that this question was concerned with worldly matters. But if we believe, as Brother Anschütz maintains, that the state will not be able to solve this problem until the churches have examined it in the light of the Gospel, then we should hurry to do our part. If it is true that the Bible is our remedy for curing the disease which today is shaking the world in a violent fever, then we must go at it right now.[147]

This tone of great urgency is common to all articles appearing in *For the Right*. But Rauschenbusch's participation at this time remained a cautious feeling-out of the situation. His answer consisted of several questions:

> First, what is the relationship of an economic order based on free competition, to the commandment "Love thy neighbor as thyself," which Brother Anschütz calls the great social idea of the Gospel? In other words, how can a person love someone else as much as he loves himself, and still compete with him?
> Secondly, how would the commandment "Love thy neighbor as thyself" influence the existence of the privileged classes if it were incorporated into the laws of the state?
> Thirdly, Brother Anschütz demands that the Gospel answer "the economic questions related to property and ownership, to work and wages." What measure does the Gospel offer to us for deciding what is rightful and what is unrightful property?

It is obvious that Rauschenbusch asked these questions only because he already had the answers. These questions clearly point to the fact that he had already progressed beyond the general, conservative position. They express rather clearly that social misery may well be the result of outward material conditions and that the gospel intends to change these injurious conditions. The commandment of neighborly love, if applied to all conditions, would change not only each human being but also society in all its aspects.

Anschütz, however, remained unaffected by these implied answers. He was able to respond to all three of these questions very well while keeping to the traditional way of thinking. Thus, he was able to come to the conclusion

> that the solution of the "social question" is not predicated on the overthrow of all existing social institutions, rather that these may go on existing unchanged, and the Gospel—through proper implantation of the right attitudes and through radical application of its commandments—would influence all social conditions in a conciliatory and enlightening way. Thus the "social question" would be as much as solved.[148]

This rebuttal now forced Rauschenbusch to clarify further his position. First he gave assurance that he himself was not intent on overthrow: "I am against the use of force, even when it means to defend what is right. I consider it as contradicting the essence of Christianity."[149] And he continued:

> I do not believe in overthrow but in development: "First the grass, then the ears, and then the kernels in the ears." I believe, just as Brother Anschütz does, that the spirit of Jesus Christ and His truth are the driving force of all human development toward the good, and that this must be true. But it seems that I have a more radical understanding of Christian truth than he does, and that I therefore expect more radical changes to occur from the application of this truth.[150]

This goes to say that for Rauschenbusch consistent application of the commandment of neighborly love would result in gradual but drastic changes, similar to the views held by socialist utopianism as expressed by Bellamy.

Then he went on to discuss the relationship of neighborly love with the notion of the competitive spirit, the pillar on which the capitalist economic system is resting, so pleasantly supported by the evolutionist principle of the survival of the fittest. Anschütz with his traditional outlook had stated that the consequences of such thinking were serving the interests of the welfare of man. He said that if two storekeepers were competitively underselling each other, the entire neighborhood would profit from this. Rauschenbusch, however, said that he would not find any friendly feelings in a storekeeper who was forced by competition to reduce his profits. And precisely the same would happen if workers were to cede their jobs to others, out of pure neighborly love, and had to starve as a consequence.

> Competition is first of all based on the fact that each man loves himself more than he loves his neighbor. Therefore, he will make every effort to wrest from the other a profit for himself. Everyone engaged in this game is almost forced to forget about others and to save his own skin. Isn't it true that the basic principle of competition is, "Love thyself more than thy neighbor"? And isn't this principle in direct contradiction to Christ's commandment?

In regard to the system of social classes, Rauschenbusch, again, could not accept a traditionalist answer. For him, Christ's commandment means giving up privileges. It is the legal expression of that Christian truth which says that we are all of the same race and that we are to love each other. "Whosoever among you wishes to be mighty, he shall be your servant." This then means that not a system of classes, but radical democracy is the fulfillment of the commandment of neighborly love.

Rauschenbusch's position regarding property has been mentioned above. He distinguished between rightful and unrightful ownership. The examples he gave in that article—land speculation or raw materials—are obvious indications of Henry George's influence on him.

### Christians Must Change Society

The above-mentioned problems are all solved in the basis that Christianity, in the commandment of neighborly love, possesses a principle which obliges it to change society and its institutions, and to change them immediately.

Anschütz proved to be an avid reader indeed. Using the example of the questionable justification of competition in regard to jobs, Rauschenbusch had borrowed an argument from Henry George. [151] Anschütz answered by using a quote from the same paragraph by Henry George:

> Those who, seeing how men are forced by competition to the extreme of human wretchedness, jump to the conclusion that competition should be abolished, are like those who, seeing a house burning down, would prohibit the use of fire. . . . Competition plays just such a part in the social organism as do those vital impulses which are beneath consciousness in the bodily organism.[152]

The most important argument used in Anschütz's rebuttal, however, was that "radical" changes in the social order would not be possible until the final victory of the gospel had become a reality. As long as there was sin in the world, the existing social order would prevail.[153]

This was precisely the same attitude which Rauschenbusch had been vigorously opposing for some time:

> I wish to register my protest against the attitude that Christianity either does not wish or cannot achieve a radical modification of present conditions.[154]

After having made this statement, Rauschenbusch is obliged to explain why Christianity should take up this mission just then. He brings out these four points: (1) The world has always been a place where injustice reigned, instead of justice. The world has always been in need of improvement, and still is:

Our present social order is like a huge woven cloth. Mankind is sitting at the ever-busy loom of time and is weaving this cloth. Every red thread of cruelty woven in, continues for a long time. It is true, the white and golden threads of justice and peace are appearing more frequently, but the pattern is still the same. This is why I maintain that the present social order, with all the good it already contains, is still in a state which requires radical changes.[155]

(2) "Christianity openly states that it has come in order to put a new order in the place of the old one." The prophet Daniel had already spoken of a new Kingdom which would destroy the old kingdoms. John the Baptist spoke of it, Christ himself declared this Kingdom to have already come, and his apostles felt that their contemporary order already belonged to the past. (3) This "revolutionary character of Christianity" had been recognized also by those who had the most to fear from its consequences: The privileged of the old order. Among the Jews, they were the "high priests, the pharisees, and the first among the people." It was they who killed Jesus. Rauschenbusch saw the same fear pervading also those who persecuted the Christians. To them the revolutionary ideas of Christianity were the more horrifying the more the representatives of these teachings declined to use force in order to bring about that new order. Christianity did not lose this revolutionary character

> until the Christians began to settle for the prevailing conditions instead of protesting against them; until they were willing to let the tree of injustice grow if only they too could partake of its fruits; until the Church had concluded that unholy treaty with Constantine and the leaders of the Church had learned to flatter the princes, instead of—like the apostle Paul—making them tremble; not until then did Samson lose his locks and his strength.

(4) A perfect new order will not be established until the coming of the Lord, but the development toward one must begin now. While Rauschenbusch would later use Christ's parables of growth in order to support this idea of his, he uses at this point his own image taken from nature:

> The development must begin before the final stage is reached; just as the development is finished at the moment when the butterfly leaves the cocoon, yet this final stage has been preceded by a week-long or often month-long development.

Those who would postpone the work of renewing society have no confidence in the present power of Christianity. Such an attitude borders on heresy:

> The worst distortion of Christianity, in relation to the individual, is the postponement of the renewal of life until the future life, not asked for and expected in this life. The worst distortion of Christianity, in relation to society is the postponement of the transformation of the social order to a future epoch instead of going about this task of the present with confidence.

Rauschenbusch, having rejected the use of force, rejected for himself the label "rebel." Regardless, Anschütz called him just that. Rauschenbusch replied:

> All right then, my brother; if you want to understand it the right way, then go ahead and call me a rebel. After all, am I not a member of the most revolutionary society the world has ever seen, the apostleship of Christ?

At this point the controversy had reached a dead end. Anschütz could do no more than repeat his well-known principles: First, that changes in society occur only indirectly, through transformations taking place within individuals; second, that a truly radical renewal of the social order will not be achieved until the second coming of Christ.[156]

In his reply Rauschenbusch added an important argument to those used before, namely, the interpretation of the contemporary situation as a time of crisis.[157] He pointed out that the introduction of steam power had led to an industrial revolution which caused definite changes in human relationships. While an artisan had actually worked together with his journeymen and these also became members of his family, the owner of a factory hardly knows his workers at all. While a customer used to discuss the product he wanted to buy with the artisan, the owner of a factory no longer knows any of his customers. Thus, essential human relationships are destroyed. The owner of a factory has no means of taking part in a happy or in a tragic event affecting his workers. He is indifferent to the human fate of those working for him; his only interest is their work. There is no longer any place, for instance, where emergency situations can be worked out in personal contact. The industrial economy has created situations which had never been foreseen by the old system of Christian ethics:

> The old rules for what constitutes a good citizen and an honest man have become insufficient. We are watching the strange spectacle that the same man may be a gentle husband, a perfect father, an active member of the congregation, a tender friend, even a praying Christian, and yet, known throughout the land as a man who pitilessly exploits small businessmen and inflates the cost of food for an entire nation, in order to enrich himself.
> 
> What we most urgently need is a restructuring of ethical teachings, an integration of the old and eternally valid principles of right and love with the changed conditions.[158]

Every Christian must cooperate in bringing about a new ethics. But above all every teacher of the people, particularly the clergy, must acquaint himself with the present problems so that he may be both a learner and a teacher at the same time and contribute to a change in the attitudes of the people. At a time when the welfare of the individual has become increasingly dependent on the welfare of the entire society, it is really the will of the people that creates better laws and a more equitable order. And the latter, in turn, offer a better chance for happiness to each human being:

> I consider it most important that we, prophets of the new order, not be found to have been merely nagging pharisees, but rather seers of the future. The people are restless. They are coming to us asking—as the people of Israel were asking the prophets—"Do you have a word of God for us?" So far they have mostly turned away from us disappointed. We were too busy with other matters. Is it to remain that way?

Once this position had been stated, the discussion of the "social question" could be considered closed. The two essential points were clearly defined. But, in *Der Sendbote*, real argumentation seemed to be only beginning. One of the older preachers wrote that one should not envy the rich since they, too, had their own problems, such as disease and similar hardships. Besides that, the preacher should not get involved in questions of "what is mine and what is thine"—Christ had done the same.[159] The first argument was answered by Rauschenbusch very simply by saying that it is true, that there were indeed many poor rich people, but many more poor poor people. The goal should be the building of a society where everyone has enough and none too much. Apart from this, the church should certainly not be a judge over wages, as Christ had refused to be judge over inheritances, but it should most certainly call wrong what is wrong.[160] If the church does not speak and act against such wrongs, others who are not guided by justice, charity, and hope will speak and act.

Nathaniel Schmidt took the same position. He also maintained that the individual was coming to feel more and more as a part of the whole. A healthy community, however, cannot exist if there are too many poor and too many rich. Such a separation on the basis of "what is mine and what is thine" completely contradicts the idea of community. This question can only be solved if the clergy in their preaching stress love and the people really defend the rights of others.[161] Still another article appeared, rejecting Henry George's proposition to abolish private ownership of real estate.[162] Other articles were published but none contained any significantly new arguments.[163]

This was the time when the editor decided to end the discussion and to give the last word to Rauschenbusch. He wrote, "It will certainly be interesting to the readers to hear a detailed presentation by the man who has worked with this question more than anyone of us."[164]

## PART II

RAUSCHENBUSCH'S DISCUSSION WITH ANSCHÜTZ AND OTHERS had been extensive and undoubtedly it was useful in solidifying his position in his own mind. When the editor of *Der Sendbote* brought the discussions to an end, Rauschenbusch wrote a clear summary of much that he had previously written.

Rauschenbusch's statement, among other things, contains a list of books which clearly shows who had influenced him most profoundly. It also shows that, up to that time, he had been little influenced in his attitude toward social problems by German theology, whether liberal or not. For this fact he as much as apologizes when he addresses his German readers:

> I am sorry that the books are mostly English books. I have not been able to get my hands on many German books, and what I did read was not what I would have recommended to my readers.
> 1. On the position of Christianity on the social question:
>    a. the Bible; especially the laws set down by Moses, the prophets, and the Gospel according to Luke.
>    b. *Social Aspects of Christianity* by Professor R. T. Ely; Prof. Ely is a personal friend of mine, a simple and serious man, a convinced Christian and one of the top experts on national economy.
> 2. On the question of land holdings. This is the fundamental problem in all social investigations. The epoch-making work on this question is *Progress and Poverty* by Henry George. It is no easy reading. The same material is presented in more readable form in *Social Problems* by Henry George. Although Henry George abandoned his attempt of establishing his own political party, his ideas are increasingly gaining recognition. Often they have been ridiculed by people who knew about them from hearsay only. But they deserve serious consideration. Henry George is a talented, honest man; he confesses his faith in God and immortality; in spite of being much maligned, his character is blameless. He is an upright opponent of socialism.
> 3. On socialism:
>    a. *Looking Backward* by Edward Bellamy. A famous book. Available also in German.
>    b. *The Fabian Essays.*

4. On free trade and protective taxes:
   a. *Problems of Today* by R. T. Ely.
   b. *Protection and Free Trade* by Henry George.
5. On the labor movement:
   *The Labor Movement in America* by R. T. Ely.
6. On the monetary question which at present is passionately discussed by the farmers, I do not know of a good book. I have not concerned myself with it very much so far.
7. Of Christian charitable activities: the highly competent book *In Darkest England* by General Booth of the Salvation Army.

Among magazines, I can recommemd *The Dawn*.

I suppose that no one will hold a grudge against me if I also recommend a monthly publication of which I am co-editor, *For the Right*.[165]

Even more important than Rauschenbusch's book list is a summary statement of his views of what Christian socialism is. Because of its intrinsic value, it is quoted in full:

### A Double Distinction

The point of view I would like our churches to adopt differs from two other positions to its right and to its left. It differs from the average Christian on the right and from the socialist and reformer on the left. It seems to me that it is not our task to anxiously seek an un-dangerous middle way, but boldly to take from both what is true and good, and to unite all in one whole, one which comes closer to the teachings of Jesus than either one of them. In my opinion, the differences are found mainly in the following points:

1. Christianity in its current form puts much emphasis on the transformation of the individual and little emphasis on the transformation of the total life of mankind. It strives to bring the individual to heaven, but not to bring heaven to earth. It preaches Paul's doctrine of righteousness, but Jesus' central doctrine of the Kingdom of Heaven on earth is half forgotten. I say, we must do the one but we must not omit the other. Christianity has, like an ellipse, two centers: the eternal life as the goal of the individual's development, and the Kingdom of God as the goal of the development of all mankind. Only one who understands these two thoughts in their full meaning and with all their interrelationships, has a complete concept of Christianity.

2. Christianity as it exists around us, points with pride to the social change, that has already been achieved through the influence of Christian endeavor, for example, the abolition of slavery, the raised position of the woman, and so forth, but it consciously refuses to tackle the remaining evils. It expects these to gradually vanish if more individuals live a true Christian life. We too believe that the unconscious influence of a life that embodies the spirit of Christ, already limits evil; but we believe that this process would be accelerated if the disciples of Jesus, with clear knowledge and inflexible will, would reveal the evils and insist that they be abolished.

3. Regarding the social evils, the Christian church restricts itself generally to an exercise of charity. That indeed mitigates the results of personal and social sins, but it does not eliminate the causes. It preaches, furthermore, repentance of sins for the individual and so attacks the causes of misery, as far as individuals are to be blamed for it. But very much of existing misery, poverty, illness, even the vices around us,

are caused by the unjust social structure. And the church, as the mouth of Christ, does not do its duty if it does not preach repentance to the state. God is not only love, he is also justice. Let justice proceed and then let love intervene in order to mitigate that misery which is still to come.
4. The Christian church has lamentably weakened Jesus' teaching on money and wealth. It protests, here and there, against too much wealth but it generally restricts itself to demanding that some of the money be used for charity. The rich man is praised and admired when he gives one tenth of his income for Christian purposes. I maintain that we first have to ask: 'Where did you get it from?' and then: 'Where is it going?' If Christian justice would be more in charge at the entrance to the depository, Christian love would manage the exit more easily.

I wrote for Christian readers, so I gave a closer look to these matters. For the same reason I will be shorter in the following points. If I were writing this article for a socialist paper, I would shorten the preceding and explain thoroughly the following, for both are equally important to me.
1. The multitude of social reformers, even if not confessedly atheistic, disregard God. They hope the abolition of all misery will come with a change of the conditions in which people live. With the Old Testament in our hands, we gladly admit the powerful influence of these external factors. But we call it a disastrous misunderstanding of the facts if the divine life, 'Christ in us,' is disregarded as the greatest power in human life.
2. The social movement is to a large extent materialistic. It demands participation in profits. They say, 'Your duties and our rights,' but we Christians must say, 'Your rights and our duties.' We are not allowed to ask anything for ourselves but everything for others. We are not hungry for profit but for justice.
3. In the socialist movement there is much hatred. They appeal to hatred and kindle it as their best ally. We reject hatred as a double edged sword without a hilt that cuts the hand of everyone who wields it. We assert, that it is possible to unite fearless resistance to injustice with prudence and love, and that this unity is more powerful than hatred.
4. A large part of the radical reform party considers violence a permissible instrument in the fight against social injustice. Christ rejected the use of violence, even for the protection of innocence. Those of us who wish to follow him unconditionally, do the same.

Of equal importance are some of Rauschenbusch's remarks on the new attitude of a Christian socialist. He answers, for instance, the question "What to do?" by urging restraint in consumption: "If you see sinfulness in modern business practices, refuse to enjoy the fruits thereof." It is the responsibility of the individual as well as the community not to throw charity at the needy, like almsgiving, but rather let them participate in what is rightfully theirs. And it is the responsibility of all to work for better laws, be it through political activities or through the right to vote.

## Articles on the Prophets

If the foregoing observations are compared with Rauschenbusch's first important book on the social gospel, *Christianity and the Social*

*Crisis*,[166] published in 1907, we see that the basic elements of that book were worked out more than fifteen years before. It is possible that he also then delineated the social aspects of the Old Testament prophets for it was about this time, around 1890-91, that Rauschenbusch "discovered" these aspects for himself. In March, 1891, *Der Sendbote* published a series of four articles by Rauschenbusch, all treating this topic.

The first of these articles contains a description of the prophetic office in general.[167] He says that the characteristic aspect of the prophet is not his ability to foretell the future, but a totally spiritual way of life. A prophet is so absolutely under the influence of God that he cannot be overcome by the magic of what is visible. This fact also determines the prophets' activities: First, they fought for the spiritual life and against a sensuous life. Second, they affirmed the spiritual life against a service of God which consists of nothing but old rituals. Inner truths are more important than outward forms. This is one of the reasons why prophets were persecuted by the priests, the guardians of tradition. Third, in the life of the state, the prophets emphasized justice as against so-called wisdom of the state. They were politicians and many of their speeches were political speeches. But they started, not with what was expedient, but what was dictated by justice. Thus they often invited the wrath of professional politicians. Fourth, the prophets felt that they were dependent solely on God. This is why they did not fear men, high or low. The fifth point is that they were men of the future:

> The future is different from the present. God sits in judgment. He guides the world safely through all the sinfulness of man, through all the seeming defeats, toward his own Kingdom. . . . The present is closer to God than the past. The future will be even closer to Him than the present. And all those in whom dwells the spirit of God have a presentiment of that which is to come. . . . Since they already now participate in the exchange and the understanding of God's future, they are able to prepare and to bring closer that same future.

It has been foretold that, in the New Covenant, the prophetic spirit of God will be the common property of the entire people of God. All Christians must be prophets; the prophetic characteristics should be the guidelines of a life in God for all Christians.

Rauschenbusch further states that a prophetic life is not mainly a life characterized by spiritual flights into higher regions. On the contrary, the suffering of the prophet is what is truly characteristic of such a man.[168] Every time a prophet gave an important word of God to men, the same spectacle repeated itself: Instead of receiving this word with an open heart, the people closed their ears and tried to close the mouth of God with all possible means. The varieties of prophetic suffering are many. Future generations, however, did accept the truth of these messages, valued them highly, and were guided by them. "This is what repeats itself from one generation to the next. Every generation honors the prophets of the past and persecutes the prophets of the present." It is true that mankind learns from the mistakes of past generations and thus makes progress. But man has never learned to hear the topical, present word of God.

> This is the way in which God elevates mankind to ever higher stages. . . . From one era to the next, mankind goes ahead urged on by the power of God, forward and upward. Prophetic men, being ahead of their times and tasting the power of the coming era, are shouting the word of God at us, the word we need today.

We can see that in this particular period Rauschenbusch finds the movement of the prophetic word through world history to represent best his idea of progress and evolution. He believed in "the presence of God in the world and in His progressive victory over the world."

> The individual develops. The community, too, develops. To believe that the first is true and to deny the second means to split apart God's work of salvation. . . . I believe, that every person is an object of divine love and respect, and a goal of divine salvation which, for him, reaches its highest fulfillment in his participation in eternal and divine life. I also believe that all of mankind is one in the eyes of God, something like an immensely huge personality that also sins, learns and progresses. And this personality, too, is a goal of divine salvation which finds its fulfillment in the perfection of the Kingdom of God on earth.[169]

This is the basis for the prophetic responsibility of the community. The spirit of God is present in the individual members of the community of God, but even more so in the community as a whole. The community as a whole has the prophetic gift and the prophetic task. The community as a whole has to be ahead of mankind in its thinking. "It has to lead that kind of life now which the other people will not lead until a future epoch has arrived." In certain ways it has done that already: (1) It has taught the world that it is wrong to consider holy places and things. God can be worshiped in any place. (2) The community has refused to recognize national barriers within its ranks, and in doing so it has led mankind on a path which will end racial hatred and nationalism.

> (3) The community of Christ was the first to defend the idea of the organic interdependence of mankind which was expressed by St. Paul in the image of a body with many parts. This presupposes the responsibility of all for all, and equally the responsibility of society to care for its weaker members. All state welfare for the poor and the sick indicates that mankind has begun to repeat, haltingly, prophetic word. The entire future restructuring of social life among the civilized nations will simply be the attempt to realize this prophetic idea in every-day life.

(4) One other Christian idea which has already found its way into the life of

society is self-sacrifice. It has been absorbed most deeply by the world of medicine, but least of all in the business world.

Rauschenbusch felt that a beginning has been made. But the community is actualizing its prophetic office only unconsciously, indirectly. It still is preoccupied with itself and employs the largest part of its energy to keep itself functioning. How much more effective could it be if it were conscious of its calling and would actualize it consciously.

In the last of these articles Rauschenbusch finally disclosed that the Baptists have a very special prophetic task.[170] His emphasis on the special Baptist contribution did not mean that he had become narrowly sectarian, for throughout his whole life, though he was a convinced Baptist,[171] at the same time he called for cooperation with all Christians. What is it that gives the Baptists a special calling? Above anything else it is the principle of absolute government by the people and of voluntary cooperation. The first is a model for the form of government all over the world, the second a model for the future form of industrial production. Baptists are more progressive than others in still another area which was as much discussed then as it is today: Women take part in the decisions of the community, even though to a lesser degree than what should be. But at least in their community structure Baptists are the most progressive. They should consider this their prophetic task, and they should joyfully propagate these attitudes.

Rauschenbusch has often been characterized as a prophet. As a young man already he felt himself to be a prophet. And he suffered the fate of all prophets: The German Baptists were those who heeded him least. For the most part they steadfastly refused to listen to his message of the social responsibility of the church. The discussion of the social question in *Der Sendbote* was soon forgotten. Later articles in *Der Sendbote* indicate that the original conservatism withstood the discussion unscathed.

## ENGLAND AND GERMANY

When the last two articles in this series were published, Rauschenbusch was no longer in America. His hearing had been more and more impaired during the two preceding years so that he was no longer able readily to carry on personal conversations. Personal pastoral care had become totally impossible for him. He felt that he was more of a burden than a source of assistance to his congregation. This is why he decided to give up his service as a preacher. He had initially hesitated to do so, waiting for the financial problems connected with construction of the new church building to be settled. But now the time had come to say goodbye. He planned to seek additional medical help in Germany in order to return to New York where he still saw future work waiting for him.[172]

His congregation refused to accept his resignation. Instead he was granted a prolong leave of absence for his trip to Germany.[173] Still not sure of what his future would be, he sailed for Germany on March 14, 1891, accompanied by his sister Emma, who at that time was studying in Boston.

First they went to England in order to get to know the Salvation Army and Fabianism.[174] After a short stopover in Hamburg, they stayed in Berlin until the end of July. From there they went to the more quiet and cool university town of Greifswald on the Baltic Sea. In both places Rauschenbusch pursued intensive studies. As astonishing as it may seem a considerable number of book slips from both university libraries have been preserved, as well as Rauschenbusch's notes which show what books he read, or at least wanted to read. I have been able to decipher about seventy titles. These are the subjects and areas in which he was most interested: The origin of the Messianic idea and of the Kingdom-of-God idea in late Judaism,[175] the life of Christ, [176] and ethics, especially in connection with statistics and sociology.[177] He also read standard history books by Ranke, Sybel and Treitschke, and the two most important books by Frederick D. Maurice.[178] He also acquainted himself with the two significant publications on the social question by Hermann Cremer.[179] Hermann Cremer was the recognized spokesman of "positive" theology, a convinced opponent of liberal theology, and the founder of the "Greifswald School." He was professor of theology at Greifswald. Rauschenbusch and Cremer's son Ernst had been friends since the time both of them had studied at the Guterloh "Gymnasium." They met again in Berlin.[180]

Some preserved letters show that for a considerable period of time his relationship with Ernst Cremer's parents had been cordial.[181] In Greifswald Rauschenbusch had stayed at the couple's home for the a week and received from them all the support he needed.[182]

Although Hermann Cremer was a staunch opponent of the liberal theologians, there was one area in which he believed, at least for a time, he could cooperate with them, namely, in the "evangelisch-sozialer Kongress."[183] Mutual Christian charity work seemed to him to be a means of overcoming their theological differences. Stocker, the preacher at the Court in Berlin, was his model: Stocker was conservative in theology, but very progressive in social areas. Many of Cremer's publications on this question are basically written in defense of Stocker. A surprisingly large number of paragraphs in these publications could really have been written by Rauschenbusch. Cremer says, for instance, that "the present social order cannot be taken as an article of faith, the same as this would not have been possible with slavery and servitude. Wherever something is found to be rotten in society, Christianity will have to be on the side of reform, although not on the side of revolution."[184] The urgency of social reforms was not new to the church:

Men with insight, especially among Christians, have long ago pointed out the dangers of the industrial development with its tendency to aggravate the contrast of rich and poor, the crowding of pennyless masses of laborers into the centers of industry, and poverty right next to the glitter of wealth.[185]

But the church had missed too many opportunities in this area, and this has led to the growth of "social democracy which is hostile toward the state and toward the church". His weightiest argument against the socialists is their materialism:

> Socialism and capitalism are brothers, grown on the same tree and both doomed to perdition since they are tied to each other by an indestructible bond. The tree is materialism, the bond is mammon.[186]

He maintained that what was required was the absorption of the Christian principle of love into the laws of the state. The Christian principle of the equality of all men was being applied widely already. In antiquity, on the contrary, the idea of equality before the law was totally unknown.

> As soon as the church had become the church of the people, and as far as even a breath of Gospel was preached and believed, the disenfranchisement of entire classes was no longer tenable. The very first influence of the Christian . . . principle of charity on the formulation of law can be seen in the abolition of that disenfranchisement.[187]

The area which so far has been least affected by this principle is the question of property:

> The principle of charity stood in stark opposition to the Roman legal concept of property, and to this day, it has not been able to transform the Roman law.[188]

These examples show that Rauschenbusch and Cremer must have easily agreed on the question of the social responsibility of the church. Both were conservative theologians; yet both believed in the possible realization of Christian love in society. For both, history furnished the proof that this realization had already begun but had not progressed far enough. Both called for changes in the social order through reform rather than revolution. It can be assumed that Cremer was Rauschenbusch's main discussion partner in Germany in 1891. How eagerly Rauschenbusch pursued such discussions can be seen in the following report by August Rauschenbusch on his son's activities:

> Walther is deeply involved with Christian-social ideas and spent most of his time in Germany getting books on these matters from the libraries in Berlin and Greifswald,

discussing them with thoughtful men and—writing a book about them, in the English language. He will soon have it published in America. This will perhaps gain him great recognition as a writer, perhaps not. He sacrificed everything else for this book.[189]

Rauschenbusch did not devote all his time to the writing of this book. He also preached sermons in Berlin and Hamburg, and his listeners are said to have been "much overwhelmed."[190]

While Rauschenbusch's mind and spirit were greatly stimulated by his German visit, his primary goal of improving his hearing was not realized. He gave up all hope of regaining his hearing. To compensate for his deafness he undertook an intensive course in lip reading in the fall.[191]

In December he finally returned to the United States. At the time of his departure from New York, he had not committed himself as to his future plans. In the fall he had received an offer to become assistant editor of the publishing company of the German Baptists in Cleveland.[192] But when he arrived in New York, he was welcomed by his congregation so enthusiastically that we may assume he refused to accept the Cleveland offer for this reason.[193] He stayed with his congregation, his only one, as their beloved pastor, until 1897 when he accepted the call of the Rochester Theological Seminary to become a teacher in the field of church history. He remained in that position until his death in 1918.

## Summary

Reviewing the documentary material given above and taking into consideration the better-known portions of Rauschenbusch's writings in *For the Right,* it becomes possible clearly to discern the outlines of Rauschenbusch's theory of social transformation through efforts of the church as his thinking developed up to and through his New York City pastorate. This theory he based on considerations which are summarized in the following paragraphs.

Especially for the poor and for the underprivileged it is difficult, if not impossible, to live a God-pleasing life in the social framework as it exists. In part, this may be explained by their personal shortcomings, but that still leaves much unanswered. Their involvement in a sinful society makes them sinners. Their struggle to stay alive makes it necessary for them to violate the basic principles of Christian ethics. Thus, the causes of their failures are the defects in the social order. For this reason individual charitable activity can no longer be the main response to human misery. The time has come when the entire social system has to be modified in such ways as to permit each human being to follow God's commandments freely.

In certain situations, individual works of charity may even in themselves violate the commandment to love one's neighbor. A case in point would be the money given to a charitable cause, if this money comes from industrial enterprises whose profits were derived from obvious exploitation of their workers. Another example is the profit from land speculation that had contributed to the impoverishment of others.[194]

The church has the duty to work for needed changes in the existing social order. If the church fails to do this, it will have to be done by others who are not motivated by love and compassion. In the message of the love of God, the church possesses the right means for the renewal of man and of mankind.

It is interesting to note how, throughout the development of his theory, Rauschenbusch insists on this double duty of individual and social salvation. He never made the mistake of simply replacing personal salvation by the call for social salvation, a mistake often made by certain of his successors. He did not need to over-emphasize to the church the need to work for personal salvation, but he had to make it very clear that evangelical concern had to include the social structures.

In Rauschenbusch's view, the greatest achievements come from a prophetic church: By being a true community and truly believing in divine justice, the prophetic church can be the model of a future improved world order. Such a church also educates the individual member of the congregation for socially oriented action. The extension of such an example and education would then necessarily result in better, more equitable social legislation and action all over the world.

Such ideas, however, require a reevaluation of the relationship of church and state. The old view of strict separation of church and state is justified, but it expresses only half of the truth. It must be the goal of Christianity to recreate the state in accordance with its highest ideals. The Kingdom of God is the ideal goal not only for the church but equally for the state.

Rauschenbusch does not appear overly shocked by the fact that ideas of this sort were not immediately and enthusiastically accepted by church members. The history of slavery serves him as a model for his own situation. There had always been people who knew that slavery was wrong and un-Christian, but they were a minority. The church herself not only kept silent but went as far as furnishing the masters of slaves with supporting biblical arguments. And yet, in the course of time, the Christian truth of the freedom inherent in man won out and resulted in the liberation of the slaves in America.[195] The same will happen in regard to the social gospel. There already are individuals who have embraced this Christian truth, but time is required before this new insight will be the common property of the church and of society at large. It will again be the church which will furnish the best counter arguments. But the history of prophecy shows that God had always, in the face of the resistance put up by the guardians of tradition, guided mankind along its way toward progress by issuing his proper prophetic words. The prophetic word is the motor power for progress in human affairs.

The Christian principle of the equality of men has gained such wide acceptance that more and more nations are instituting democratic governments. Now the chances for a radical renewal of society are also much greater, since all people now have the right to participate in the framing of state laws. The real defect in the existing system consists in the fact that the very idea of democracy has not yet penetrated the economic order.

The path of society which leads to the Kingdom of God, that is, the path toward the Christianization of society, is radical democratization. As in nature, according to the laws of evolution, progress is inevitable, so also progress in the social order cannot be stopped. A certain trend is already emerging. All that the church is required to do is to help open the gates to the future of God, instead of leaving the future to knock at its gates from outside. The proclamation of this good news is the prophetic task of the church. The history of Christianity itself foreshadows the right path.[196]

But as early as 1892, Rauschenbusch gave up his conviction that progress was inevitable.[197] However, he did not change his view that radical democratization was the proper way toward the establishment of the Kingdom of God on earth. This conviction he defended throughout his life. In the last section of his last book, he again wrote of this connection between the Kingdom of God and political democracy:

> The Cross of Christ contributes to the strengthening of the power of prophetic religion, and therewith the redemptive forces of the Kingdom of God. Before the Reformation, the prophet had only a precarious foothold within the Church, and no right to live outside of it. The rise of free religion and political democracy has given him a field and a task. The era of prophetic and democratic Christianity has just begun. This concerns the social gospel, for the social gospel is the voice of prophecy in modern life.[198]

This view of relating politics and religion within the idea of the Kingdom of God was clearly conceived by Rauschenbusch in his early years and maintained through his life. It finally became the focal point of Rauschenbusch's most important critic, Reinhold Niebuhr.[199]

Rauschenbusch, in his early years, was most decisively influenced by Henry George. As soon as Edward McGlynn was able freely to defend Henry George's ideas, Rauschenbusch as well as many other reformers of that time, became fascinated by this man's thinking.[200] He believed that many of George's ideas were to be found in the Bible also.[201] Many of these ideas he defended publicly as soon as George's books were published. But the time came when Rauschenbusch felt that George was too much of an individualist. George was unable to see society as an organism, as did Rauschenbusch. And this was the reason why George did not see the necessity for radical changes in the social order.[202] In this point, Rauschenbusch was much more in sympathy with the socialists, although he rejected their materialistic attitudes, their hostility toward religion and, above all, their views on the use of force in the social struggle. Rauschenbusch saw the best means for bringing about a better future in a proper combination of socialism and Christianity. "The Brotherhood of the Kingdom," in which Rauschenbusch played a leading role, saw as its main task the bringing into being this proper combination.[203]

It is not surprising to see that in this situation Rauschenbusch did not find much interest in European Continental socialism. He was much more interested in the events taking place in England. There, one generation earlier, Frederick Maurice had conceived the idea of combining Christian socialism with the concept of the Kingdom of God. And there, in Fabianism, a reawakening of Christian socialism was taking place before his eyes. He was also interested to see that Booth and the Salvation Army were experimenting with new ways of social work.[204] Except for Bellamy's American socialism, it was in the main by ideas coming from England that Rauschenbusch was most strongly influenced.[205]

Rauschenbusch also read Mazzini and there found some support for his view of social progress as a growing realization of Christian principles. We are also told that Rauschenbusch was reading Tolstoy's *My Religion* in that period,[206] a book whose radical Christianity was exercising a strong influence on the development of the social gospel in America.[207]

Rauschenbusch's concept of a prophetic character of Christianity remained unchanged even later. He was always happy to find books which presented similar views. He freely quoted such views if they could lend support to his own theses. But the origin of these theories is found in the period of his five-year service as preacher in New York. When he went to Germany, before the age of thirty, he was no longer searching for answers but only for confirmations. These confirmations, strangely enough, he received mainly from the conservative theologian Albrecht Ritschl, and not from liberal quarters.

His relationship to Ritschl, however, is not as clearly discernible as we would wish it to be. He mentions Ritschl for the first time in July 1892.[208] Before that time, the name Ritschl does not appear anywhere. And yet, Rauschenbusch had used the famous simile of the ellipse with two focal points—one personal salvation, the other the Kingdom of God[209]— for the first time in January 1891, that is, long before there was anything like a Ritschlian School in America.[210]

Christianity has, like an ellipse, two centers: the eternal life as the goal of the individual development and the Kingdom of God as the goal of the development of all mankind.²¹¹

This formulation is much too typical to be a chance occurrence only. Rauschenbusch's own position forced him to reach just such a conclusion. In his congregation, his main task was to save souls. As a citizen of New York, he saw his task as that of influencing the community as a whole and to change it in accordance with biblical guidelines. In spite of this it is difficult to decide whether Rauschenbusch's independent spirit had been touched and influenced by Ritschl or whether he had recognized in Ritschl a kindred spirit and therefore used his simile.

An essential prerequisite for Rauschenbusch's entire development was his theological independence. His skeptical attitude toward the Old Testament made it possible for him to discover independently the significance of the prophets. And it was this independent thinking in matters of theology which made it possible for him to combine his religiosity with the social problem. It was this openness of his which was more important for the development of his social gospel than all outward influences he had encountered.

# LIST OF RESOURCES

*Walter Rauschenbusch's published articles, 1884-1891*

"Baptist Mission Work in Germany," *National Baptist*, Philadelphia (July 31, 1884).

"Review of 'Der Index der Verbotenen Bücher, Ein Beitrag zur Kirchen—und Literaturgeschichte, von Dr. Fr. Heinrich Reusch, Bonn 1883 und 1885,'" *The Baptist Quarterly Review* (October 1886) 564-567.

"Das Fussaschen" *Der Sendbote* (January 26, 1887).

"Zehn goldene Regln für junge Christen," *Der Sendbote* (February 16, 1887).

"Review of 'Die Geschichte der beiden Märtyrer Adolf Clarenbach und Peter Fliesteden, nach gleichzeitigen städtischen und landesherrlichen Urkniden und aus wieder aufgefundenen Druckschriften erzählt von Carl Krafft, Elberfeld, 1886,'" *The Baptist Quarterly Review* (April 1887) 275f.

"Für die Glieder der Jugendvereine," *Der Sendbote* (May 11, 1887).

"Bericht aus Newark, N.J.," *Der Sendbote* (May 18, 1887).

"Warum Glauben? Predigt über Matthäi 9, 29," pamphlet, Cleveland 1887.

"Eastern Conference of the German Baptist," *The Standard*, Chicago (September 1887).

"The Importance of the Proper Education of Our German Population," address read on October 27, 1887, *New York Baptist Annual, 1888*.

"Einweihung in Boston, Mass.," *Der Sendbote* (November 16, 1887).

"The Waldenses," *American Baptist*, St. Louis (1888).

"Mancherlei Gaben und ein Geist," *Der Sendbote* (January 18, 1888).

"Dr. Edward Judson über Traktatverbreitung," *Der Sendbote* (February 22, 1888).

"The Savings Efficiency of Money," *The Christian Inquirer*, New York (May 24, 1888).

"Du sollst nicht stehlen," *Der Sendbote* (July 18, 1888).

"Beneath the Glitter," *The Christian Inquirer* (August 2, 1888).

"Impressions of the Northfield Meetings, *The Christian Inquirer* (August 16, 1888).

"Der Gebrauch der Stimme in der öffentlichen Rede," *Der Hülfsobote*, Stettin, Germany (October 1888).

"Die vier Evangelisten, Matthäus," *Der Sendbote* (October 31, 1888).

"Die vier Evangelisten, Markus," *Der Sendbote* (November 7, 1888).

"Die vier Evangelisten, Lukas," *Der Sendbote* (November 14, 1888).

"Die vier Evangelisten, Johannes," *Der Sendbote* (November 21, 1888).

"Who Shall Educate? Church or State?" *Seventh Annual Session of the Baptist Congress, 1888*, 28-31.

"On Immigration" *Seventh Annual Session of the Baptist Congress, 1888*, 86f.

"Shall the Christian Academies Go?" *National Baptist* (January 17, 1889).

"Die Liederdichter der Baptisten," *Der Sendbote* (January 9, 1889).

"Des Missionars Berufung," *Der Sendbote* (January 16, 1889).

"High Rent and Low Morals," *National Baptist* (March 1889).

"Schlagen oder tragen?" *Der Sendbote* (March 27, 1889).

"That Boston Fad," *The Christian Inquirer* (August 15, 1889).

"Report of the Committee on the Telugu Missions," *Baptist Mission Magazine* (July 1889).

"The Condition of the Churches as seen among the Foreign Populations," *The New York Baptist Annual, 1890,* 38-41.

"Influence of Mazzini," *Colloquium* (November 1889).

"Natural and Artificial Monopolies," *Eighth Annual Session of the Baptist Congress, 1889,* 55-61.

"Relation of Church and State," *Eighth Annual Session of the Baptist Congress, 1889,* 143-145.

"Notes on the Dancing Question," *Colloquium* (April 1890).

"Review of Social Aspects of Christianity, by Richard T. Ely," *Colloquium* (April 1890).

"Einweihung in der Zweiten Gemeinde, New York," *Der Sendbote* (April 16, 1890).

"What Changes in Society are Necessary?" *Colloquium* (July 1890).

"Die sociale Frage," *Der Sendbote* (July 16, 1890).

"Die sociale Frage," *Der Sendbote* (August 13, 1890).

"Die sociale Frage," *Der Sendbote* (September 24, 1890).

"Die sociale Frage," *Der Sendbote* (October 15, 1890).

"Die sociale Frage," *Der Sendbote* (November 5, 1890).

"State Insurance in Germany," *National Baptist* (December 1890).

"Noch einmal die sociale Frage," *Der Sendbote* (January 28, 1891).

"Das prophetische Amt," *Der Sendbote* (March 4, 1891).

"Das prophetische Leiden," *Der Sendbote* (March 11, 1891).

"Die prophetische Mission der Gemeinde Christi," *Der Sendbote* (March 18, 1891).

"Die prophetischen Aufgaben der Baptistengemeinden," *Der Sendbote* (March 25, 1891).

Not included are Rauschenbusch's contributions in *For the Right*, and his Sunday school lections.

*Other works by Rauschenbusch, mentioned in this paper:*

*Neue Lieder, Ubersetzungen von Ira D. Sankey's "Gospel Hymns No. 5,"* New York, 1889.

*The Righteousness of the Kingdom*, edited and introduced by Max L. Stackhouse. Nashville, 1968.

"A Conquering Idea," *The Examiner* (July 21, 1892).

*What shall we do with the Germans?* Pamphlet, 1897.

*Leben und Wirken von August Rauschenbusch*. August Rauschenbusch, completed by his son Walter Rauschenbusch. Kassel, 1901.

"Dogmatic and Practical Socialism," *Rochester Herald* (March 14, 1901).

"Why I am a Baptist," *Rochester Baptist Monthly* (November 1905-March 1906).

"The Influence of Historical Studies on Theology," *American Journal of Theology* (1907) 111-127.

*Christianity and the Social Crisis.* New York, 1907.
*For God and the People: Prayers for the Social Awakening.* Boston, 1910.
*Christianizing the Social Order.* New York, 1912.
*A Theology for the Social Gospel.* New York, 1917.
"The Genesis of 'Christianity and the Social Crisis,'" *The Rochester Theological Seminary Bulletin: The Record* (November, 1918) 51-53.

## Secondary Sources

Aaron I. Abell (ed.), *American Catholic Thought on Social Questions.* Indianapolis, 1968.

John R. Aiken, "Walter Rauschenbusch and Education for Reform," *Church History* (December 1967) 456-469.

Ray Stannard Baker, *The Spiritual Unrest.* New York, 1910.

Charles Albro Barker, *Henry George.* New York, 1955.

Sherman B. Barnes, "Walter Rauschenbusch as Historian," *Foundations* (Summer 1969) 263-272.

Vernon P. Bodein, *The Social Gospel of Walter Rauschenbusch and Its Relation to Religious Education.* New Haven, 1944.

Dietrich Bonhoeffer, *Gesammelte Werke,* vol. I. Munchen, 1958.

Henry W. Bowden, "Walter Rauschenbusch and American Church History," *Foundations* (Summer 1966) 234-250.

Olive J. Brose, *Frederick Denison Maurice.* Ohio University Press, 1971.

Ernst Cremer, *Hermann Cremer. Ein Lebensbild.* Gütersloh, 1912.

Hermann Cremer, *Die Fortdauer der Geistesgaben in der Kirche.* Gütersloh, 1890.

_____ *Uber den Einfluss des christlichen Princips der Liebe auf die Rechtsbildung und Gesetzgebung.* Griefswald, 1889.

Torben Christensen, *Origin and History of Christian Socialism, 1848-1854.* Aarhus, 1962.

Robert D. Cross, "Introduction to the Torchbook edition of *Christianity and the Social Crisis,*" New York, 1964.

Joseph Martin Dawson, *Baptists and the American Republic.* Nashville, 1956.

James Dombrowski, *The Early Days of Christian Socialism in America.* New York, 1936.

Edwin Emerson, *A History of the Nineteenth Century,* vol. III. New York, 1902.

Henry George, *Progress and Poverty.* New York, 1958.

_____ *Protection or Free Trade.* New York, 1940.

Robert T. Handy, *The Social Gospel in America, 1870-1920.* New York, 1966.

Berverly Harrison, "Review of 'The Righteousness of the Kingdom,'" *Social Action* (May 1969) 34f.

Richard Hofstadter, *Social Darwinism in American Thought.* Revised edition, Boston: The Beacon Press, 1955.

C. Howard Hopkins, *The Rise of the Social Gospel in American Protestantism 1865-1915.* New Haven, 1940.

Frederic M. Hudson, "The Reign of the New Humanity," unpublished Ph.D. dissertation, Columbia University, 1968.

Winthrop S. Hudson, *The Great Tradition of the American Churches*. Revised edition, New York, 1963.

────── *How American Is Religion in America: Reinterpretation in American Church History*, Jerald C. Bauer (ed.). Chicago, 1968, 153-167.

Benson Y. Landis, *A Rauschenbusch Reader*. New York, 1957.

Frederick Denison Maurice, *The Kingdom of Christ*, 2 vols. London, 1959.

────── *The Gospel of the Kingdom of Heaven*. 3rd. edition, New York, 1888.

────── *The Life of Frederick Denison Maurice, Chiefly Told in His Own Letters; Edited by his Son Frederik*. 2 vols., New York, 1884.

Henry F. May, *Protestant Churches and Industrial America*. New York, 1949.

Donald B. Meyer, *The Protestant Search for Political Realism, 1919-1941*. Berkeley, 1961.

F. W. C. Meyer, "Walter Rauschenbusch, Preacher, Professor and Prophet," *The Standard* (February 3, 1911).

────── "Walter Rauschenbusch," *Bulletin of the German Department of the Rochester Theological Seminary, Jubiläumsausgabe* (July, 1927) 47-50.

Conrad Henry Moehlman, "The Life and Writings of Walter Rauschenbusch," *Colgate-Rochester Divinity School Bulletin* (October 1928) 32-37.

Reinhart Müller, *Walter Rauschenbusch: Ein Beitrag zur Begegnung des deutschen und des amerikanischen Protestantismus*. Leiden, 1957. Worthy of attention.

Allan Nevins, *Study in Power: John D. Rockefeller, Industrialist and Philanthropist*. 2 vols, New York, 1953.

A. H. Newman, *A History of the Baptist Churches in the United States*. 3rd edition, New York, 1900.

Emma Rauschenbusch-Clough, *Social Christianity in the Orient*. New York, 1914.

Albrecht Ritschl, *The Christian Doctrine of Justification and Reconciliation*. 2nd edition, Edinburgh, 1902.

Dores R. Sharpe, *Walter Rauschenbusch*. New York, 1942.

Donovan E. Smucker, "The Origins of Walter Rauschenbusch's Social Ethics," unpublished Ph.D. dissertation, University of Chicago, 1957.

────── "The Rauschenbusch Story," *Foundations* (January 1959) 4-12.

Max L. Stackhouse, "The Formation of a Prophet: Reflections on the Early Sermons of Walter Rauschenbusch," *Andover Newton Quarterly* (January, 1969) 137-159.

Syndor L. Stealy, *A Baptist Treasury*. New York, 1958.

## Footnotes

1. Benson Y. Landis, ed., *A Rauschenbusch Reader: The Kingdom of God and the Social Gospel* (New York, 1957).
2. Robert T. Handy, ed., *The Social Gospel in America, 1870-1920* (New York, 1966).
3. Walter Rauschenbusch, *The Righteousness of the Kingdom*, edited by Max L. Stackhouse (Nashville, 1968).
4. Henry W. Bowden engaged in a study of classroom notes, taken by one of Rauschenbusch's students 1911-1913: "Walter Rauschenbusch and American Church History," *Foundations*, Summer, 1966, 234-250. John R. Aiken investigated Rauschenbusch's involvement in an educational crisis in Rochester 1908: "Walter Rauschenbusch and Education for Reform," *Church History*, December, 1967, 456-469. More examples will follow.
5. *Social Action*, May, 1969, 34f.
6. Dietrich Bonhoeffer, *Gesammelte Werke*, edited by Eberhard Bethge (Munchen, 1958) I, 101, 104-112.
7. Reinhart Müller, *Walter Rauschenbusch, Ein Beitrag zur Begegnung des deutschen und des amerikanischen Protestantismus* (Leiden, 1957).
8. Ray Stannard Baker, "The Spiritual Unrest," *American Magazine*, December, 1909, 176-183. In a book with the same title (New York 1910) 260-285.
9. Dores Robinson Sharpe, *Walter Rauschenbusch* (New York 1942).
10. Vernon P. Bodein, *The Social Gospel of Walter Rauschenbusch and Its Relation to Religious Education* (New Haven, 1944).
11. Robert D. Cross, in his introduction to the Torchbook edition of *Walter Rauschenbusch, Christianity and the Social Crisis* (hereafter "CSC") (New York, 1964) places the publication of the journal *For the Right* by mistake after Rauschenbusch's trip to Europe, 1891 (see p. xii).
12. August Rauschenbusch (hereafter A.R.), Correspondence, October 20, 1882, in archive of North American Baptist Seminary (hereafter NABS), Sioux Falls, catalogue No. 21. About August Rauschenbusch, cf. Walter Rauschenbusch, *Leben und Wirken von August Rauschenbusch*, autobiography, completed by his son (Kassel, 1901); Müller, *op. cit.*, 9-12.
13. "Ein Jubelfest der zweiten Gemeinde in New York," *Der Sendbote*, June 23, 1886.
14. Sharpe, 59.
15. A. R., "Noch einige Nachrichten von der Schule in Rochester," *Der Sendbote*, April 21, 1886.
16. Walter Rauschenbusch (hereafter W.R.), Correspondence, July 13, 1886, NABS No. 848.
17. Sharpe, 60.
18. W.R., Correspondence, March 20, 1886, NABS No. 127.
19. W.R., Correspondence, June 22, 1886, NABS No. 850.
20. W.R., Correspondence, July 14, 1886, NABS No. 849.
21. W.R., Correspondence, July 13, 1886, NABS No. 848.
22. *Ibid.*
23. *Ibid.*
24. F.W.C. Meyer, "Walter Rauschenbusch," *Bulletin of the German Department of the Rochester Theological Seminary, Jubiläumsausgabe*," July 1927, 48.
25. W.R., Correspondence, July 13, 1886, NABS No. 48.
26. *Ibid.*
27. *The Life of Frederick Denison Maurice; Chiefly Told in His Own Letters; Edited by His Son Frederick*, 2 vols. (New York, 1884) I, 176-178; cf. the 15-page long dedication in: Maurice, *The Kingdom of Christ*, 2 vols. (London, 1959). Olive J. Brose, *Frederick Denison Maurice*, Ohio University Press, 1971, presents a new view on the relation between Maurice and Coleridge, 23-27.
28. "Life of Maurice," *op. cit.*, vol. II, pp. 515f.
29. W.R., "Review of *Der Index der verbotenen Bücher. Ein Beitrag zur Kirchen—und Literaturgeschichte* by Fr. Heinrich Reusch," in *The Baptist Quarterly Review*, October, 1886, 275f.
30. W.R., "Baptist Mission Work in Germany," *National Baptist*, Philadelphia, July 31, 1884.
31. W.R., "Review of *Die Geschichte der beiden Märtyrer Adolf Clarenbach und Peter Fliesteden*, by Carl Krafft," in *The Baptist Quarterly Review*, April, 1887, 275f.
32. W.R., Correspondence, April 12, 1887, NABS No. 64.
33. Frederic M. Hudson also indicates Rauschenbusch's early preference of church history: "The Reign of the New Humanity," unpublished Ph.D. dissertation, Columbia University, 1968, 26.
34. W.R., Correspondence, September 24, 1886, NABS No. 821.
35. Mission reports by Emma Rauschenbusch: *Der Sendbote*, January 5, 1887; May 2, 1888. Emma became Dr. Clough's second wife in 1894 and published later his autobiography with the significant title: *Social Christianity in the Orient, by John E. Clough, written down for him by his wife Emma Rauschenbusch-Clough* (New York, 1914).
36. A.R., Correspondence, September 25, 1886, NABS No. 17.
37. F.W.C. Meyer, "Walter Rauschenbusch, Preacher, Professor and Prophet," *The Standard*, February 3, 1911.
38. F.W.C. Meyer, *Bulletin*, 1927, *op. cit.*, 48.
39. Conrad Henry Moehlman, "The Life and Writings of Walter Rauschenbusch," *The Colgate Rochester Divinity School Bulletin*, October, 1928, 33; Bodein, 3; Sharpe, 58.
40. This more moderate view is held by Joseph Martin Dawson, *Baptists and the American Republic* (Nashville, 1956) 177.
41. W.R., Correspondence, September 24, 1886, NABS No. 821.
42. A.R., Correspondence, September 25, 1886, NABS No. 17.
43. W.R., Correspondence, September 24, 1886, NABS No. 821.
44. *Der Sendbote*, November 10, 1886.

45. Sharpe, 21.
46. A.R., Correspondence, August 9, 1877, NABS No. 46.
47. A.R., Correspondence, ca. October 1882, NABS No. 22.
48. A.R., Correspondence, September 25, 1886, NABS No. 17.
49. W.R., Correspondence, March 12, 1888, NABS No. 57; A.R., Correspondence, November 10, 1891, NABS No. 43.
50. Letter by Benjamin O. True to W.R., January 29, 1889, in "D.R. Sharpe Collection," American Baptist Historical Society Archives, Rochester. About A.R.'s research, cf. article "August Rauschenbusch," *Mennonitisches Lexikon*, (Karlsruhe [Baden]) 1958, Vol. 3, 430-432.
51. So did Donovan E. Smucker, "The Rauschenbusch Story", *Foundations*, January 1959, 4.
52. W.R., Correspondence, January 14, 1887, NABS No. 55.
53. W.R., Correspondence, December 14, 1886, NABS No. 52.
54. *Der Sendbote*, December 8, 1886, 388.
55. W.R., Correspondence, January 14, 1887, NABS No. 55.
56. W.R., "Das Fusswaschen," *Der Sendbote*, January 26, 1887.
57. W.R., "Für die Glieder der Jugendvereine," *Der Sendbote*, May 11, 1887. W.R. usually signed his articles with his full name. But there is an article, "Zehn goldene Regeln für junge Christen," *Der Sendbote*, February 16, 1887, signed only with "W.R.," which might have been written by him at that time.
58. W.R., "The Genesis of 'Christianity and the Social Crisis,'" *The Rochester Theological Seminary Bulletin: The Record*, November 1918, 51; cf. Max L. Stackhouse, "The Formation of a Prophet," *Andover Newton Quarterly*, January, 1969, 137-159; 142, n. 19.
59. Sharpe, 41.
60. Letter by Hanna to W.R., January 10, 1887, NABS No. 967; cf. article "Hanna," *New Catholic Encyclopedia* (New York, 1967) Vol. 6, 914f.
61. Letter by Ernst Cremer to W.R., September 22, 1886, in "D.R. Sharpe Collection." More letters by Ernst Cremer are in the NABS archive.
62. W.R., *Christianizing the Social Order* (New York, 1912 [hereafter CSO]) 394.
63. Stackhouse, "Formation" *op. cit.*, 143.
64. CSO, 91-92.
65. Aaron I. Abell, ed., *American Catholic Thought on Social Questions* (Indianapolis, 1968) 162.
66. Henry George in his *The Standard*, May 7, 1887.
67. W.R. Correspondence, March 12, 1887, NABS no. 64.
68. Stackhouse. "Formation," 137, 155 and passim.
69. *Ibid.*, 141f.
70. W.R., "Warum Glauben," in his scrapbook in D.R. Sharpe Collection, *Sermons*, Vol. VII, 168-180, preached on October 23, 1887.
71. *Ibid.*, 6.
72. *Ibid.*, 14.
73. W.R., "Mancherlei Gaben und ein Geist," *Der Sendbote*, January 18, 1888.

74. W.R., Correspondence, August 18, 1887, NABS No. 59.
75. W.R., Correspondence, May 31, 1887, NABS No. 823.
76. W.R., "Beneath the Glitter," *Christian Inquirer*, New York, August 2, 1888, cited in Sharpe, 81f.
77. W.R., "The Savings Efficacy of Money," *Christian Inquirer*, May 24, 1888; cf. Bodein, 5.
78. Stackhouse notes in his bibliography that the manuscript is now misplaced: *Righteousness*, 306.
79. Cited in Sharpe, 80.
80. Published in *American Baptist* (St. Louis, 1888).
81. Cf. Sherman B. Barnes, "Walter Rauschenbusch as Historian," *Foundations*, Summer 1969, 254-262; 255 and n. 8. Besides classroom notes he mentions an address, October 16, 1890, and a sermon in August 1893.
82. Handy, in his introduction of W.R., "Conception of Missions": "Because of his intense concern for the social question, Rauschenbusch's continuing interest in missions has often been overlooked," *Social Gospel, op. cit.*, 268.
83. W.R. translated one of her poems from English into German to publish it in *Der Sendbote*: W.R., Correspondence, July 14, 1886, NABS No. 849.
84. The first of the scrapbooks of Rauschenbusch material, made by W.R. himself, now in the D.R. Sharpe Collection, contains on the first page a number of poems by W.R. One with the title "Fass, Vater, meine Hand," was published in Hamburg, 1889. His most famous poem became "The Little Gate to God," 1918: *The Record*, November 1918, 39f; Sharpe, 451f.
85. The first collection of translations of English gospel songs originated in 1889: *Neue Lieder, Übersetzungen von Ira D. Sankey's "Gospel Hymns No. 5"* (New York, 1889). W.R. translated about half of these songs. Additional collections were written by him in 1897 and 1907, last published *Evangeliums-Sänger 1, 2 und 3* (Kassel, 1931). The prayers, partially published in *The American Magazine*, 1909, are combined in *For God and the People. Prayers of the Social Awakening* (Boston, 1910).
86. W.R. wrote an essay about "Hymns of Social Redemption," which ends with the following words: "If the Church has old hymns of social redemption stored away, let us have them. If not, let us make new ones. But social redemption wants hymns." *The Record*, November 1918, 12. For the hardly noticed relations between the social gospel and the hymns of the church cf. Horton Davies, "The Expression of the Social Gospel in Worship," *Studia Liturgica*, Summer 1963, 174-192.
87. "The Record," November 1918, pp. 51f.
88. W.R., "Mancherlei Gaben und ein Geist," *Der Sendbote*, January 18, 1888. Spencer's organic interpretation of society began to appeal to progressive American clergy, cf. Richard Hofstadter, "Social Darwinism in American Thought (revised edition, Boston 1955) chap. 6. W.R. mentions Spencer only once, very

early: "That Boston Fad," *The Christian Inquirer*, August 15, 1888. He might have learned about him by reading George, cf. Henry George, *Progress and Poverty* (New York, 1958) esp. 517.
89. W.R., "Du sollst nicht stehlen," *Der Sendbote*, July 18, 1888.
90. In a letter by Hanna to W.R., April 9, 1887, NABS No. 968, quoting a letter by W.R. In a time when Rauschenbusch was already much more in favor of Socialism, this letter was written: "I am glad that you continue to think about Socialism. . . . It will not be the final word in God's history but *now* it is a duty which lies before mankind and its moral leaders. Your plan to inform slowly is the best. Single ardent sermons don't help much— especially with slow thinking people. Don't throw the wisdom to the people from above. But sit with them together and think. To put a question mark in the heads of young people is a lasting work." W.R. to Max Leuschner, December 23, 1903, quoted in: Donovan E. Smucker, "The Origins of Walter Rauschenbusch's Social Ethics," unpublished Ph.D. dissertation, University of Chicago, 1957, 79.
91. W.R., "Die vier Evangelisten," *Der Sendbote*: "Matthäus," October 31; "Markus," November 7; "Lukas," November 14; "Johannes," November 21, 1888.
92. It is difficult to tell when this friendship began. Rauschenbusch preached the ordination-sermon for Nathaniel Schmidt in the spring of 1888: Stackhouse, *Formation*, 146-148.
93. An extensive study of the "Brotherhood" is Frederic Hudson's "The Reign of the New Humanity," *op. cit.*
94. W.R., Correspondence, December 12, 1888, NABS No. 57.
95. Letter by W.R., June 11, 1888, published in *Der Sendbote*.
96. Postcard by Strong to W.R., March 6, 1889, D.R. Sharpe Collection.
97. *Der Sendbote*, June 30, 1897.
98. Details from: Edwin Emerson, Jr. *A History of the Nineteenth Century* (New York, 1902) 1692.
99. W.R., Correspondence, December 12, 1888, NABS No. 57.
100. *Ibid.*
101. W.R., "Impressions of the Northfield Meetings," *The Christian Inquirer*, August 16, 1888.
102. W.R., "Who Shall Educate? Church or State?" *Seventh Annual Session of the Baptist Congress*, 1888, 28-31.
103. *Ibid.*
104. Norman Fox, "The Church and the State," *The Christian Inquirer*, 1888.
105. W.R., newspaper clipping, in scrapbook, D.R. Sharpe Collection.
106. Stackhouse, *Formation*, 144.
107. W.R., before the Baptist Social Union of New York, March 1889, newspaper clipping in scrapbook, D.R. Sharpe Collection; cf. W.R., "What Shall We Do with the Germans," 1897, NABS No. 271.
108. W.R., in *Seventh Annual Session of the Baptist Congress*, 1888, 87. Two more contributions of W.R. about immigrant churches in this time are: "Condition of the Church as seen among the Foreign Population" (October 29, 1889) *The New York Baptist Annual 1890*, 38-41; W.R., "German Baptists and Theological Education," mentioned in: W.R., "Aus Rochester," *Der Sendbote*, December 17, 1890.
109. *Baptist Mission Magazine*, July 1889, 184-187.
110. W.R., "Dr. Edward Judson über Traktatverbreitung," *Der Sendbote*, February 22, 1888; W.R., "Des Missionars Berufung," *ibid.*, January 16, 1889, containing a translation of the poem "The Missionary's Call" by Nathan Brown. He found this poem in: Henry Burrage, *Baptist Hymn Writers and Their Hymns.* He reported about this book in *Der Sendbote*: "Die Liederdichter der Baptisten," January 9, 1889.
111. W.R., "Bericht von der östlichen Konferenz," *Der Sendbote*, October 9, 1889. He wrote in this function "An die Gemeinden der östlichen Konferenz," *Der Sendbote*, January 1, 1890.
112. Cf. CSO, 93: "In 1891 I spent a year of study in Germany, partly on the teaching of Jesus, and partly on sociology."
113. W.R., "High Rents and Low Morals," *National Baptist*, March, 1889.
114. *Ibid.*: "I think it's real hard to be good, when there is no back yard."
115. Stackhouse, *Formation*, mentions two sermons about this theme. "Rauschenbusch's nascent social radicalism had been born of Biblical conservatism and pastoral concern. It was also bound by these. He was deeply troubled by the violence which was being advocated by some. He recognized in many instances that blood was the price of progress and that change might not be possible without it. Yet he could not advocate bloodshed. The cross was for him still stronger then the sword." 158.
116. *Ibid.*, 151f.
117. W.R., "That Boston Fad," *The Christian Inquirer*, August 15, 1889. It is already evident that Rauschenbusch was more sympathetic toward Bellamy's "American" socialism, than toward the continental form.
118. Sharpe, 68.
119. W.R., Correspondence, March 11, 1889, NABS No. 91.
120. W.R., Correspondence, July 4, 1889, NABS No. 48.
121. Sharpe, 47.
122. Allen Nevins, *Study in Power: John D. Rockefeller, Industrialist and Philanthropist* (New York, 1953) Vol. II, 88f.
123. Letter by Bessie to W.R., May 6, 1889, D.R. Sharpe Collection.
124. W.R., "Aus der Zweiten Gemeinde, New York," *Der Sendbote*, December 18, 1889. The D.R. Sharpe Collection contains four letters by Rockefeller to W.R., dated May 20, November 26 and 29, 1889, and March 3, 1890. Regarding Rockefeller's conditions, cf. Nevins, *op. cit.*, vol. II, 157: "Rockefeller wished to give to well-established or established causes and institutions; to give in a way, that would stimulate other gifts and enlist numerous supporters; to give to undertakings that would persist after his support was removed; and to give for subjects not merely sound, but the soundest within the range of his investigations." The Baptist Education Socie-

ty, which led to the University of Chicago, was probably created to meet these ideas: cf. A.H. Newman, *A History of the Baptist Churches in the United States* (3 edition, New York, 1900) 477. Rockefeller also contributed to the German Department of the Seminary in Rochester (W.R., "Aus Rochester," *Der Sendbote,* December 17, 1890) and to the Baptist Seminary in Germany.
125. W.R., "Einweihung in der Zweiten Gemeinde, New York," *Der Sendbote,* April 16, 1890.
126. An introduction to the cornerstone laying still exists: NABS No. 865; cf. *Der Sendbote,* October 30, 1889.
127. W.R., "Einweihung" etc., *op. cit.*
128. W.R., Correspondence, December 17, 1889, NABS No. 49.
129. "Die 9. Bundeskonferenz," *Der Sendbote,* October 9, 1889.
130. Sharpe, 71.
131. The first issue of this paper is probably lost. The scrapbooks in the D.R. Sharpe Collection contain an editorial by W.R., reprinted in Bodein, 9f, and his article "Where does it all come from?"
132. Cf. John R. Aiken, "Walter Rauschenbusch and Education for Reform," *op. cit.,* 465f.
133. *Eighth Annual Session of the Baptist Congress,* 1889, 54f.
134. W.R., "Natural and Artificial Monopolies," *ibid.,* 55-61. Page 55 is reprinted in *Rauschenbusch Reader, Op. cit.,* 138-143.
135. *Ibid.,* 56.
136. *Ibid.,* 60.
137. W.R., "Relation of Church and State," *ibid.,* 138-140; reprinted in *Rauschenbusch Reader,* 143-145.
138. Frederic M. Hudson, "The Reign of the New Humanity," *op. cit.,* 48.
139. *Life of . . . Maurice . . ." op. cit.,* II, 137f; cf. II, 575 and Frederick Denison Maurice, *The Gospel of the Kingdom of Heaven* (3rd edition, New York, 1888) 122.
140. This has only recently been shown: Torben Christensen, *Origin and History of Christian Socialism, 1848-1854* (Denmark: Aarhus, 1962) passim.
141. This expression by Hudson, "The Reign of the New Humanity," 48, appears to me to be well aimed.
142. E. Anschütz, "Die sociale Frage," *Der Sendbote,* June 18, 1890.
143. Cf. Henry F. May, "Conservative Social Christianity," *Protestant Churches and Industrial America* (New York, 1949) Part IV, 1, 163-169; Charles Howard Hopkins, "The Church Challenges Socialism," *The Rise of the Social Gospel in American Protestantism, 1865-1915* (New Haven, 1940) IV, 67-78.
144. So "Die Arbeiterbewegung," *Der Sendbote,* June 9, 1886.
145. "Pater McGlynn das neue Evangelium," *Der Sendbote,* August 10, 1887.
146. W.R., "Die sociale Frage," *Der Sendbote,* August 13, 1890.
147. W.R., "Die sociale Frage," *Der Sendbote,* July 16, 1890.
148. E. Anschütz, "Die sociale Frage," *Der Sendbote,* July 30, 1890.
149. W.R., "Die sociale Frage," *Der Sendbote,* August 13, 1890.
150. *Ibid.*
151. Henry George, *Protection or Free Trade* (New York, 1949) 306.
152. *Ibid.,* 307.
153. E. Anschütz, "Die sociale Frage," *Der Sendbote,* August 27, 1890.
154. W.R., "Die sociale Frage," *Der Sendbote,* September 24, 1890.
155. *Ibid.*
156. E. Anschütz, "Die sociale Frage," *Der Sendbote,* October 22, 1890.
157. W.R., "Die sociale Frage," *Der Sendbote,* November 5, 1890.
158. *Ibid.*
159. A Henrich, "Die sociale Frage," *Der Sendbote,* September 24, 1890.
160. W.R., "Die sociale Frage," *Der Sendbote,* October 15, 1890.
161. Nathaniel Schmidt, "Das Mein und Dein," *Der Sendbote,* October 29, 1890.
162. F.A. Kemsies, "Die social Frage," *Der Sendbote,* October 1, 1890.
163. C.A. Daniel, "Welche Stellung sollen wir, als Gemeinde, der socialen Frage gegenüber einnehmen?" *Der Sendbote,* December 10, 1890. (Daniel was a friend of Rauschenbusch since they were together in the seminary and he became minister in Harlem in 1890.) T.J. Kötzli, "Zur socialen Frage," *Der Sendbote,* January 1 and 7, 1891.
164. Editorial in *Der Sendbote,* January 7, 1891.
165. Walter Rauschenbusch (hereafter "WR"), "Noch einmal die sociale Frage," January 28, 1891.
166. W. R., *Christianity and the Social Crisis* 1907).
167. W. R., "Das prophetische Amt," *Der Sendbote,* March 4, 1891.
168. W. R., "Das prophetische Leiden," *Der Sendbote,* March 11, 1891.
169. W. R., "Die prophetische Mission der Gemeinde Christi," *Der Sendbote,* March 18. 1891.
170. W. R., "Die prophetische Aufgabe der Baptistengemeinden," *Der Sendbote,* March 25, 1891.
171. cf. W. R., "Why I am a Baptist," *Rochester Baptist Monthly,* November, 1905; March, 1906, reprinted in *Colgate Rochester Divinity School Bulletin,* December, 1938. Sydnor L. Stealy, *A Baptist Treasury* (New York, 1958) introduces a revised reprint of these articles: "It is one of the best statements ever written on our distinctive principles." p. 163.
172. A rough copy of a letter by W. R., declaring his resignation, still exists: North American Baptist Seminary (hereafter "NABS") No. 846.
173. Editorial, *Der Sendbote,* February 25, 1891.
174. Dores Robinson Sharpe, *Walter Rauschenbusch* (New York, 1942) 68; Vernon P. Bodein, *The Social Gospel of Walter Rauschenbusch and Its Relation to Religious Education* (New Haven, 1944) 28; Cf. W. R., *The Righteousness of the Kingdom,* 233.
175. H. Jolowicz, *Die Himmelfahrt des Propheten Jesaja;* A. Dillmann, *Das Buch Henoch;* Ed. Riehm, *Die messianische Weissagung;* Rich. Clemens, *Die Offenbarungen der Propheten Henoch, Esra und Jesaja;* Georg H. A. Ewald,

*Die Geschichte des Volkes Israel bis Christus;* Carl Scholl, *Die Messias-Sagen des Morgenlandes;* H. von Corodi, *Kritische Geschichte des Chiliasmus;* Jos. Beck, *Uber die Entwicklung und Darstellung der messianischen Idee;* Joh. Jac. Broix, *Über den Ursprung und die allmähliche Entwicklung des Messianismus;* Th. Bredow, *Das Reich dieser Welt und das Reich Gottes;* Richard Whately, *The Kingdom of Christ;* Carl August Hase, *Neue Propheten.*
176. Karl Hase, "Leben Jesu," in *Gesammelte Werke*, vol 4; cf. *Christianity and the Social Crisis* (hereafter "CSC") 46; Carl Th. Keim, *Die Geschichte Jesu von Nazara;* Joh. August W. Neander, *Das Leben Christi;* J. R. Seeley, *Ecce Homo;* Berhard Weiss, *Lehrbuch des biblischen Theologie des Neuen Testamentes;* F. Delitzsch, *Jesus und Hillel;* August Satori, *Die Stellung Jesu zu den Parteien seiner Zeit.*
177. K. F. Ständlin, *Geschichte der Sittenlehre Jesu;* Bernhard Wendt, *Kirchliche Ethik vom Standpunkt der christlichen Frieheit;* Adolph Wagner, *Die Gesetzmässigkeit in den scheinbar willaürlichen Handlungen vom Standpunkt der Statistik;* Alexander von Oettingen, *Die Moralstatistik in ihrer Bedeutung für eine christliche Sozialethik;* Albert Schäffle, *Bau und Leben des socialen Körpers* (This book caught his interest in particular—he quoted it often; *Righteousness*, 154, 161, 171f; "The Ideals of Social Reformers", AJSoc (September 1896) 210; "Das kollektive Leben der Menschheit," unpublished manuscript in D. R. Sharpe Collection, p. 9.
178. Frederick Denison Maurice, *The Kingdom of Christ*, and *Theological Essays.*
179. Hermann Cremer, *Über den Einfluss des christlichen Princips der Liebe auf die Rechtsbildung und Gesetzgebung* (Greifswald, 1889) and *Die Fortdauer der Geistesgaben in der Kirche* (Gütersloh, 1890).
180. W. R., Correspondence, July 22, 1891, NABS No. 128.
181. A letter by Ernst Cremer to W. R. refers to an existing correspondence between W. R. and Ernst Cremer's parents. September 1, 1887, NABS No. 890.
182. W. R., Correspondence, July 22, 1891, NABS No. 128.
183. The following: Ernst Cremer, *Hermann Cremer: Ein Lebensbild* (Gütersloh 1912) chapter 12.
184. *Ibid.*, 191.
185. *Ibid.*, 185.
186. *Ibid.*, 187f.
187. Hermann Cremer, *Über den Einfluss op.cit.*, 16f.
188. *Ibid.*, 25.
189. A. R., Correspondence, November 1891, NABS No. 43.
190. *Ibid.*
191. W. R., Correspondence, October 14, 1891, NABS No. 58.
192. "Die Sudwestliche Konferenz," *Der Sendbote*, October 7, 1891.
193. "Zweite deutsche Baptisten-Gemeinde in New York," *Der Sendbote*, January 6, 1892; Cf. Editorial, *Ibid;* Sharpe, *op. cit.*, 69f.
194. This essential realization did not keep Rauschenbusch from asking Rockefeller to contribute to his church. Even later he was very successful in raising funds for the Seminary.
195. W. R. used this example often. Rauschenbusch neglected the race question, but even there he was prophetic. He said in 1909: "A solution of the labor question so thorough that it would be possible to hand over entire industries to the black race without evoking industrial hostility, would offer a solid hope to the negro," in "The Sagamore Sociological Conference," 1909, p. 12.
196. This was made clear in March 18, 1891 in *Der Sendbote*, March 18, 1891. Cf. W.R's later definition of prophecy: "The only safe form of prophesying is to prolong the curve of the past," in "The Influence of Historical Studies on Theology", *AJTh* (1907) 111-127.
197. W. R., "The Conceptions of Missions," *The Watchman*, December 1, 1892, reprinted in Handy, *Social Gospel*, 268-273; cf. Winthrop Hudson, *The Great Traditions of the American Churches* (revised edition, New York, 1963) 228.
198. W. R., *A Theology for the Social Gospel* (New York, 1917) 279.
199. Cf. Donald B. Meyer, *The Protestant Search for Political Realism, 1919-1941* (Berkeley: 1961) 260.
200. C. A. Daniel, a companion of W. R. since his early years, remembers: "Walter Rauschenbusch soon entered into the interest of the common people, became interested in social welfare of the people, made an ardent study of social ideals, the Kingdom of God, and the book of Henry George, *Progress and Poverty*. Henry George and Father Glynn were a great force among the multitudes and the idea of the Kingdom of God gripped Walter's soul," "Some reminiscences of my friend Walter Rauschenbusch," NABS No. 820, p. 6.
201. Cf. Rauschenbusch's definition property with that from Henry George, *Progress and Poverty*, *op. cit.*, 334: "As a man belongs to himself, so his labor when put in concrete form belongs to him."
202. Charles Albro Barker, *Henry George* (New York 1955) 509: "Henry George, with only the slightest waverings of inconsistency, had always been a pro-capitalist thinker.... He was always conservative as to our . . . institutions of church and state." Rauschenbusch called the single-taxers "new-school individualists" in "Dogmatic and Practical Socialism," reprinted in Handy, *Social Gospel*, 308-322.
203. Frederic Hudson, "New Humanity."
204. Sharpe, *op. cit.*, reports Rauschenbusch's disappointment about the Salvation Army, p. 427.
205. The English influence on the American social gospel is noted by Winthrop S. Hudson: "How American Is Religion in America?" in *Reinterpretation in American Church History*, Jerald C. Bauer (ed.) (Chicago, 1968) 153-167.
206. Sharpe, *op. cit.*, 83f; Bodein, *op. cit.*, 5.
207. Tolstoi's views have been propagated in America particularly by the "Christian Commonwealth Community"; cf. James Dombrowski, "The Early Days of Christian

Socialism in America," New York, 1936, chap. XII.
208. W. R., "A Conquering Idea," *The Examiner*, July 21, 1892.
209. Albrecht Ritschl, *The Christian Doctrine of Justification and Reconciliation*, (2 edition, Edinburgh: 1902) 11.
210. The main representatives of Ritschlian theology in America, William Adams Brown and William Newton Clarke, had not yet written their books. Clarke became the most important theologian of the "Brotherhood of the Kingdom."
211. Walter Rauschenbusch, "Noch einmal die sociale Frage," *Der Sendbote*, January 28, 1891, cf. p. 69.

P 692